Cats

Grace Pond & Angela Sayer

John Bartholomew & Son Limited
Edinburgh

First published in Great Britain 1976 *by*
JOHN BARTHOLOMEW & SON LIMITED
12 Duncan Street, Edinburgh EH9 1TA
Reprinted 1982, 1984

ISBN 0 7028 1061 4

Designed and illustrated by Allard Design Group Limited
Printed in Great Britain by John Bartholomew & Son Limited

Contents

Introduction to cats

How, when, or where the domestic cat first evolved is still very much a matter of conjecture, but as a rule zoologists agree that it all started more than fifty million years ago in the Eocene period, with the miacis, a small weasel-like creature. From this creature many families, such as the dogs, the bears, and the civets evolved, and it is from the last that the *Felidae,* or felines, gradually developed. Eventually there were more than fifty distinct species, ranging from the tigers, lions, leopards, and cheetahs right down to the small jungle and desert cats, the margays, and lastly, but certainly not least, the domestic cat.

All have common characteristics, and with one or two notable exceptions, have longish tails. They are digitagrade, walking on their toes, with the padded paws making for silent hunting. The claws are retractile, that is, they can be drawn in and out at will, even those of the cheetah, which can be drawn in but lack the full skin protection other felines have.

The skulls are rounded ; the hearing is acute except in the case of some white cats ; the ears are used as parabolas. They cannot see in complete darkness but the contraction of the pupils, varying according to the amount of light available, enables them to see in a very dim light.

The felines are carnivorous or flesh eaters, using their thirty adult teeth in a scissor-like action to tear their food apart. The tongue covered with small hooks or papillae is used like a rasp to clean flesh off bones.

The intricate muscle system enables all the cats to jump and climb, while the whiskers are connected to sensitive nerves which act as an additional sense when hunting or creeping through small spaces.

The fur, both in length and thickness, varies considerably, as do the coat patterns. It is thought the tail may act as a balance when climbing, but it is definitely used to express various moods, being swished violently from side to side in anger and twitching with annoyance.

So much for the make-up of the cat, but how it became domesticated is still not known. It is thought that it was the result of inter-breeding between the smaller caffre and jungle cats of North Africa, which became domesticated through living in close proximity to humans. There is no doubt that at least four thousand years ago they were being worshipped as gods by the

5

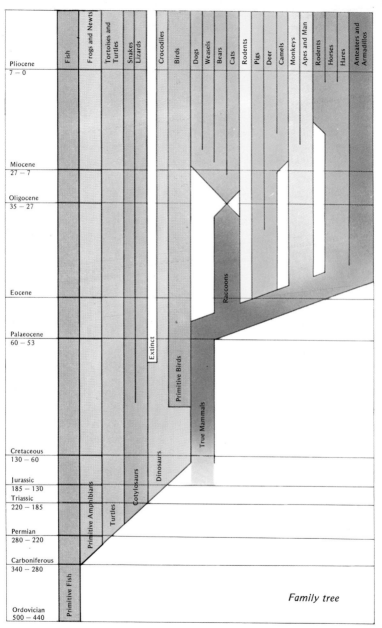

Family tree

Period	Dates
Pliocene	7 – 0
Miocene	27 – 7
Oligocene	35 – 27
Eocene	
Palaeocene	60 – 53
Cretaceous	130 – 60
Jurassic	185 – 130
Triassic	220 – 185
Permian	280 – 220
Carboniferous	340 – 280
Ordovician	500 – 440

Fish
Frogs and Newts
Tortoises and Turtles
Snakes
Lizards
Crocodiles
Birds
Dogs
Weasels
Bears
Cats
Rodents
Pigs
Deer
Camels
Monkeys
Apes and Man
Rodents
Horses
Hares
Anteaters and Armadillos
Raccoons
Extinct
Primitive Birds
True Mammals
Dinosaurs
Cotylosaurs
Turtles
Primitive Amphibians
Primitive Fish

Egyptians and soon most families owned at least one, believing they were a form of protection against evil, but also regarding them with affection. This is evident from the many beautiful little statuettes and models of cats the Egyptians left behind. They were depicted in wall paintings, and used as decorations on rings, necklaces and other items of jewellery.

On the death of a cat the whole family went into mourning and the body was mummified, often being wrapped in costly linens, and placed in highly ornamented and sometimes bejewelled cases of metal or wood, with maybe a mummified mouse for company.

There is also early mention of the cat in India and China, and a little later in Japan, and eventually the cat came to Europe. The Romans are given credit for introducing it into Britain, while in A.D. 936 Howel the Good, a Welsh prince, made a number of laws giving the domestic cat legal protection. By the Middle Ages, however, the cat had come to be treated with abhorrence, being thought of as witches' familiars and in league with the devil. Before long they were threatened with extinction, but gradually the wheel turned again until in Victorian times it was the fashion to have a 'cat on the mat', especially one of the more exotic long-haired varieties brought over from France.

1871 saw the birth and eventual spread of the Cat Fancy throughout the world after the first official cat show, the brain child of Harrison Weir, was held at the Crystal Palace. The show attracted so much attention that others followed in rapid succession.

Society went in for pedigree cats in a big way, with Queen Victoria owning a Blue Persian, and visiting cat shows accompanied by Edward, Prince of Wales. At first, cat breeding was the prerogative of the rich, some of whom owned as many as fifty cats and travelled to shows all over the country with a retinue of servants.

Cat clubs were formed, and the National Cat Club became the first registering body, keeping a National Register of Cats and holding shows under its sponsorship. In 1910 the National Cat Club gave up these rights, but still remained the premier club, and the Governing Council of the Cat Fancy came into being.

The council is composed of delegates elected each year by members of all the affiliated cat clubs and societies in Great Britain. Briefly it registers and transfers cats; classifies cat breeds; approves new standards and grants prefixes. Shows are held under its jurisdiction, at which it grants challenge and premier certificates.

Cat Fancies are run on much the same lines throughout the world.

Kitten

Choosing the right cat

Having decided that a kitten is the right pet for you, and that its care during normal times and holidays will not present any major problems, it must be determined whether it is to be a mongrel or a pedigree, long-haired or shorthaired, male or female. The upkeep of any kitten, whatever its lineage or background, will cost roughly the same amount, but a poorly reared or unthrifty animal may cost a great deal in veterinary fees at the beginning, so this is a point to bear in mind. Showing cats can be a very pleasant hobby and shows do have special sections for neutered pedigree cats of both sexes; therefore, even if you do not wish to take up cat breeding, a pedigree kitten could start you on a new hobby and introduce you to the whole new world of the Cat Fancy.

Mongrel kittens are always very appealing and can be obtained from the local pet shop, from friends whose cat has had an unwanted litter, or from the animal welfare societies which are always wanting homes for stray or abandoned animals. Pedigree cats can be found through advertisements in the local papers or in the periodicals devoted to Fancy Cats, or by contacting the breed societies. A visit to a large Championship Cat Show enables one to see all sorts of pedigree cats and kittens and to chat with their owners, but it is not advisable to buy a kitten at the show, as it may possibly have picked up an infection on the day. If you cannot resist buying one, however, pay your deposit, and arrange to collect him two or three weeks later. If he does become sick, he stands a much better chance of a quick recovery with his breeder and litter-mates than he would in his new home.

Different breeds have quite different characteristics and it is important to select the right kitten for your home, family, temperament, and mode of life. If possible, have two kittens rather than one, for you will get more than twice the enjoyment and some breeds need company and companionship almost as much as they need food and warmth. Cats are always happier in pairs when in boarding catteries or left alone for any length of time, and cats brought up with other animals seem to develop fewer neuroses, and are easier to handle than cats reared in solitary conditions.

Whether pedigree or mongrel, the points to look for in choosing your kitten are the same. Firstly, make sure that the kitten has been properly weaned and has lived completely apart from its mother for at least a week. Many breeders say that kittens are weaned when they are capable of eating solids, forgetting that a large proportion

9

of their nourishment is still being drawn from the dam's milk, and the kitten, upon being taken to its new home, will lose an alarming amount of weight during the first couple of weeks — a serious setback in such a tiny creature at a critical stage in its development. Secondly, the kitten should have a healthy appearance with no sign of the pot-belly which could denote the presence of worms, and should have received two doses of worming medicine prescribed by a veterinary surgeon prior to weaning. The eyes should be bright without any signs of discharge or inflammation. The inside of the ears should be clean without any trace of black grittiness which could be canker. A check inside the mouth should reveal a pink and healthy state of the tongue and gums and sharp white baby teeth.

The coat must be clean and not have any blackish-brown grits among the hairs. These are flea excreta and are easier to spot than the very active fleas. There should be no sores or scabs anywhere on the body. Lift the tail and make sure there is no staining on the fur which could mean that the kitten suffers from diarrhoea, and check that the coat and breath do not have an unpleasant odour.

If possible, see the kittens at play; they will soon settle down after becoming accustomed to your presence. Choose the kitten that appeals to you the most and looks the most active and healthy. If it is a pedigree kitten, discuss with the breeder the purposes for which you require the kitten and be guided by him if your aim is to show or breed. As a pet, it does not really matter whether you pick a male or female, as the neutering operations are simple matters these days and can be carried out before the kitten reaches breeding age. If breeding is your aim, buy only a female kitten, or maybe two, which, when adult, can be taken to suitable stud males for mating. Never buy a male and female with the intention of setting up a breeding pair of cats. Cats do not live naturally in a monogamous state, and the keeping of stud males is a job for the experts.

If the kitten you choose has not been vaccinated against Feline Infectious Enteritis, it is advisable to get this done as soon as possible, certainly before he comes into contact with any other cats. It is preferable to ask the breeder to get this done and then call again to collect your kitten after the immunity has developed.

Always take a carrier in which to take home your new pet. There are many types on the market, wickerwork, fibre-glass, mesh, perspex, and so on, and if it is your intention to show or breed or to take your cat on visits in the car, it is well worth investing at the

A basket designed to carry a cat easily and comfortably

outset in a good lightweight carrier big enough for an adult cat. Failing this, excellent disposable cardboard carriers are available in pet stores and from some animal welfare societies for very little cost, and are quite suitable for collecting your kitten, and for the odd visit to the veterinary surgery or to boarding kennels. Do not take your kitten out of the carrier until safely in his new home, no matter how loudly he protests at his confinement. Try to arrange to collect him when you will have a couple of days to spare to get him settled in.

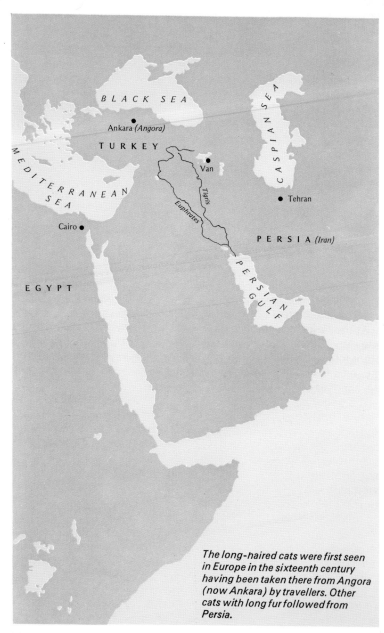

The long-haired cats were first seen in Europe in the sixteenth century having been taken there from Angora (now Ankara) by travellers. Other cats with long fur followed from Persia.

The breeds

It is thought that the original domestic cats were short-coated, having evolved several thousand years ago from the jungle and desert cats of North Africa, but the cats with long coats have very little history. It is known that they were first seen in Europe in the sixteenth century having been taken there from Angora (now Ankara) in Turkey by travellers and possibly sailors. Other cats with long fur followed from Persia, but how their coats originated, or how long they had been in existence is not known. It is presumed that it happened by a chance mutation which was perpetuated through in-breeding amongst cats living in a confined area, such as around the Van Lake in Turkey, where the very nature of the country would make far-afield wandering for cats difficult. It is apparent that these cats were, and still are, much admired and treasured by the Turks. It did not occur to them that the cats could be of general interest and it was not until quite recently that there was any attempt at planned breeding, nor were any records kept.

The first official cat show held in Britain, in 1871, made a terrific impact on the public and was responsible for the beginning of world-wide interest in breeding cats of specific colours.

At the first show there were classes for Blacks, Whites, Tabbies and Any Other Colour Angoras and Persians, but they were far outnumbered by the short-hairs. In a few years, however, the numbers of the long-hairs increased and they soon outnumbered the short-haired cats being exhibited.

The original Angoras (as the cats from Turkey were called) had narrow heads, tall ears, longish noses and bodies, while the Persians were said to have broader heads, shorter noses, smaller ears, cobbier bodies, and longer fur. Cross-breeding was tried, and eventually the varieties were so mixed up that no one could tell one from the other, at least that is what one writer wrote at the beginning of the twentieth century. It is, however, significant that for many years all Long-hairs were known as Persians.

Little was understood about selective breeding, but very soon fanciers began to appreciate that by using specific cats with certain colourings, it was possible to produce many different varieties. They also realized that to reproduce certain characteristics a great deal depended on the pedigree, but it took many years to produce cats of the outstanding type seen today. The general standard for long-hairs set by the Governing Council of the Cat Fancy is for the head to be broad and round, with good width between the small well-set ears. The nose should be short and broad, the cheeks round and full, and the eyes large and round. The dense long coat should be soft and silky, never woolly in texture : the body should be cobby on short sturdy legs, and the tail should be short and full, with no kinks. The fur around the head should be extra long, being brushed up to form a frame for the face.

The long-hairs recognized and given breed numbers are :

1	Black	7	Silver Tabby
2	White (blue eyes)	8	Brown Tabby
2a	White (orange eyes)	9	Red Tabby
2b	White (odd eyes)	10	Chinchilla
3	Blue	11	Tortoiseshell
4	Red Self	12	Tortoiseshell and White
5	Cream	12a	Bi-Coloured
6	Smoke	13	Blue Cream
		13b	Colourpoint

Also recognized are the Birmans (13c) and the Turkish (13d), but their type is more that of the original Angoras (see separate items).

Any Other Colour also has a number, i.e. 13a, but of course no standard is given for this, as it used to register new varieties that have not yet been given recognition, for cats with new coat patterns that have appeared by accident, and so on.

Long-hair Black

Black Long-hairs

One of the oldest varieties, but the Blacks have never appeared at the shows in great numbers, although those that are seen are often outstanding, with beautiful dense black coats and large deep orange-coloured eyes. They have several times been Best in Show.

A reason for the comparative scarcity of this variety may be that the kittens when young often have rusty-greyish coats, showing little promise of the glossy jet-black fur that comes with adulthood. It is difficult to realize that frequently the kitten with the rustiest coat becomes a magnificent champion.

The fully-grown Black should have dense jet-black fur, with no white hairs or brown shading. The type is the same as other long-hairs with the eyes being deep orange or copper in colour.

The fur reacts quickly to strong sunlight or damp, by turning brown. Any cat that is to be shown should not be allowed to sit for long periods in the sun and should be kept indoors when it is raining.

Blacks may be used in breeding Whites, Smokes, Bi-Colours, and Tortoiseshells. They may be bred from Tortoiseshells, from Blacks mated to Blacks, to Creams, to Whites, and possibly Tabbies.

Some fanciers advocate an occasional crossing with a Blue to keep the type. It is a well-known fact that many of the famous Black champions had blue breeding in the pedigrees.

White Long-hairs

There are now three recognized varieties of White Long-hairs, the blue-eyed, the orange-eyed and the odd-eyed. It is said that the original Angora cats were white with blue eyes, and a number were exhibited at the early shows. However, because the Persian type came to be preferred, cross-matings with cats of other colours were tried, with the result that the blue eye colouring was frequently lost, and more Whites with orange eyes were born. Both varieties appeared in the same class at the shows and more often than not the Whites with the orange eyes won, which upset the owners of blue-eyed cats. To please everyone, both varieties were given championship status and separate classes.

Resulting from the cross-breeding, cats were also born with eyes of different colours, i.e. odd-eyed, having one eye blue and the other orange. Some of these cats had very good type and it was found that they could be used to produce cats with blue eyes, with orange eyes, and with odd-eyes, but not always to order. Some years ago they too were given a class of their own but were not granted championship status at that time, but, realizing the important part they could play in breeding blue-eyed Whites, this has now been granted. Certain strains of blue-eyed white cats are deaf, but it is very unusual for a white cat with orange eyes to be deaf. It is said that an odd-eyed White may be deaf on the blue side but have good hearing on the orange-eye side.

The Whites with orange eyes have increased rapidly in numbers over the years with many excellent examples appearing at the shows, often winning the coveted title of Best in Show. The blue-eyed Whites are also improving in type, and some striking cats have been exhibited; this is also true of those with odd-eyes.

Long-hair White

The kittens when newly born may have a pinkish appearance until the fur starts to grow. As all kittens have blue eyes at first, it may be difficult for the first month or two to tell what the ultimate eye colouring will be. The odd-eyes are comparatively easier to pick out in the litter at an early age: one eye will differ from the other as the orange tinge appears. The kitten that still has deep-blue eyes when about nine weeks old will probably keep that colouring.

White kittens are now very popular and there is a constant demand for them as pets, as well as for breeding.

Blue Long-hairs

A champion Blue is an excellent example of what to look for when choosing a kitten that will come close to the set standard. It is one of the most popular of the long-haired varieties. The fur may be of any shade of blue, but must be of the same even colour throughout right down to the roots. The big round eyes should be a deep orange or copper in colour.

Blues appeared at the first shows as 'Any Other Variety' as most had white or tabby markings in their coats. In 1889 they were given a class of their own: 'Blue — Self-Coloured — without white', and from that time have been shown in ever increasing numbers. Faults are white hairs in the coat, a pale or brownish frill, and a kink in the tail.

As the type can be so outstanding, Blues have been used over the years to improve many of the other long-haired varieties, namely the Blacks, Whites, and Creams, and also to produce new varieties, such as the Colourpoints.

When first born, Blue kittens may have shadow tabby markings which disappear with the growth of the fur. Frequently the more marked the kitten, the better it may be when adult. Lively and gay, the Blue kittens are most photogenic, often appearing on chocolate boxes and Christmas cards.

Red Self

One of the rarest long-haired varieties and one of the most difficult to produce completely self, that is, the same deep rich-red colour all over with no tabby markings at all. Invariably markings do appear somewhere, particularly on the head. Of the 100 points in the set standard, 50 are given for the coat alone, which should be as described above with no white hairs. The large round eyes should be a deep-copper colour.

They were first seen at the shows many years ago, but in those days were referred to as 'Orange, marked and unmarked', appearing in the same classes as those we now call Red Tabbies. The type is frequently very good, the heads being very broad and the noses short and broad.

There is a fallacy that all red cats are males. This is not true : when both the parents are pure-red bred, the kittens may be male and female. This is also true in the case of the Red Tabbies.

Long-hair Red Self

Cream Long-hairs

The Creams appeared at the early cat shows as 'Fawns' which was a fair description of their colouring in those days. Apparently they were 'sports' in Orange and Red litters and were considered of no value for breeding, being sold as pets. The story is very different today with the Creams rivalling the Blues in popularity.

The fur should be a pale- to medium-Cream colour right down to the roots, without shadings or markings, fifty points being given for the colour, coat, and condition in the standard. The eyes should be a deep-copper colour. The type is usually very good. The fur must not be harsh in texture, nor reddish in colour, a fault referred to as 'hot'.

Creams are used to produce Blue-Creams (see Blues and Blue-Creams) but an occasional cross with a Blue is recommended by some fanciers to help keep the type.

The kittens are most attractive, pale-cream balls of fluff, which are always much admired at the shows.

Smokes

One of the most striking of all the long-haired varieties, referred to frequently as 'the cat of contrasts'. In the adult the coat may at first appear to be black, but as the cat moves glimpses of the white undercoat may be seen gleaming like silver. The face should be jet black with a silver frill, as should be the ear tufts. The body colouring should be black, shading to silver on the sides and flanks, the undercoat being as white as possible; the feet should be black. The eyes may be orange or copper in colour. The type is usually very good.

The kittens are black when first born, and it may be very difficult for a novice to assess their potentialities for some months, although experienced breeders are usually able to detect minute white markings in the fur while they are still very young. These markings indicate that the kittens are Smokes. Frequently a beginner registers a kitten as a Black, only to realize, after a month or so, that it is in fact a Smoke.

Smoke may be mated to a Smoke, but they may also result from crosses with Blacks. A Silver Tabby should not be used as this could mean tabby markings appearing which would be difficult to breed out. Using Blues it is possible to have Blue Smokes which are also recognized, the colour 'blue' replacing 'black' in the recognized standard. The contrast between the top and undercoats is not quite so great, but the Blue Smokes are very attractive.

Grooming is all-important to present a Smoke at its best. The undercoat should be brushed up so that it gleams through the top coat. Like Blacks, the coats react strongly to sunlight and damp, and if a cat is to be exhibited, care should be taken to ensure that this does not happen.

Long-hair Cream

The Tabbies

There are three varieties of Tabby colourings recognized in Britain, the Silver, the Brown, and the Red. All should have the same pattern of contrasting markings. There should be delicate pencillings on the face, giving the appearance of spectacles around the eyes, with swirls on the cheeks, and an 'M' mark on the forehead. Around the chest should be two unbroken necklaces, known as the 'Lord Mayor's Chains', and looking down on the shoulders the distinct markings should take the shape of a butterfly. The tail and legs should be ringed, with the flanks and saddle also having deep bands of the contrasting colour. The markings should stand out clearly from the background colour, but are sometimes very difficult to see in the long flowing fur.

Brown Tabby

The first long-haireds seen in Europe were said to be self-coloured and it is thought that the tabby markings were introduced through crossing with the short-haired tabbies. The Brown Tabbies appeared at the shows in the early 1900s with the classes being well filled, but gradually the numbers decreased until today it is a comparatively rare variety.

The colour should be a rich tawny sable with black tabby markings standing out distinctly. Grooming plays an important part in this so that the pattern of markings may be clearly seen. The eyes may be hazel or copper in colour. The type is not always as good as many other varieties, but outstanding cats have appeared from time to time. Faults are a white chin, a white tip to the tail, and brindling in the coat, that is, hairs of a wrong shade appearing in the correct colouring.

As there are so few Brown Tabbies it may be difficult to know what stud to use. Breeders have produced outstanding cats by crossings with Blacks, Blues, Torties, and Blue Creams. A Red Tabby should not be used, nor a Silver Tabby, as these do not help the colouring or the markings.

Silver Tabby

This is another variety which was once very popular but the numbers have dropped considerably over the years. At first the Silvers had no definite pattern of markings and the ground colouring was bluish, but careful breeding over the years has produced striking cats with pale-silver coats and jet-black markings. In striving to perfect the Silver Tabbies, the early

Long-hair Tabbies

fanciers produced Shaded Silvers and the Chinchillas.

The ground colour should be a pure, pale silver with jet-black markings. Any brown tinges or blurring of the markings are considered faults. The eyes may be green or hazel in colour. The type should be as for other long-hairs, but is not always of a very high standard. It is difficult to find suitable studs for matings to improve the variety. Silver Tabby can be mated to Silver Tabby but if used indefinitely may result in loss of type. Both Blacks and Blues have been advocated, but a Brown Tabby should never be used.

The kittens are born dark and it may be several months before the true pattern of markings can be clearly seen. It is said that the darker the kitten at birth, the better the coat and markings when adult.

Red Tabby

A variety that is always much admired with fur of deep rich-red colour, with even deeper red tabby markings and eyes of deep-copper colour. The Red Tabbies appeared at the early shows in the same class as the Brown Tabbies, but very few had the correct markings, and most had white chins and white tips to tails, which are definite faults. In recent years the type and colour has improved, but it is still difficult to produce a cat with the correct pattern of backings which stand out clearly from the background colour.

Red may be mated to Red but eventually this may lead to loss of type and markings. Blacks and Tortoiseshells are used, as are Red Selfs, but it is still difficult to produce a cat with perfect markings.

The fur is usually very silky, and careful grooming is required to present the cat looking its best. Some fanciers use Fuller's earth sprinkled well into the coat and brushed well out to make the fur stand up; others give the cats warm bran baths, rubbing this well into the coat and then brushing completely out.

Chinchillas

Considered by some to be one of the most beautiful varieties with the distinctive pure-white fur tipped with black giving a sparkling silver appearance. They appeared at the end of the last century, apparently as the result of cross-breeding Silver Tabbies and Blues, as early writers speak of a bluish coat. By 1900 Chinchillas were bred with heavy and light tickings, and it was decided at the time that the cats with darker tickings should be known as Shaded Silvers. However, there was such confusion as to when a dark Chinchilla became a Shaded Silver and vice versa, that within a year or two the Shaded Silver standard was dropped in Britain, although it is still recognized in many other parts of the world.

The standard says that the undercoat should be pure white, with the back, flanks, head, ears, and tail being tipped with black. The legs have slight tippings, but the chin, ear tufts, stomach and chest should be pure white. The tip of the nose should be brick red and the eyes should be rimmed with black or dark brown. The eyes should be emerald or blue-green in colour. Faults are a pale-pink nose, too heavy tickings, bars, and brown or yellow tinges in the coat.

The kittens are dark when first born, often with tabby markings on the back and sides, and shadow rings on the tail. These markings vanish as the fur grows and frequently the darkest kitten grows up to be the cat with the most sparkling coat.

The Chinchillas are slightly finer boned than most other long-hairs, and as yet are not quite so typey, but some beautiful specimens can be seen at the shows. They are frequently in the public eye, appearing in advertisements both in the press and on television, and there is a constant demand for the kittens.

Long-hair Chinchillas

The Tortoiseshell and the Tortoiseshell-and-White Long-hairs

These are two of the female-only varieties, any males born are invariably sterile. It is for this reason that they have very little history. It is known that they were seen at the early shows having been produced more or less by chance.

The Tortoiseshell should have a coat of black, red, and cream, well broken into patches. The colours should be bright and the patches should be quite distinct from one another. The type is as for other long-hairs, with fifty points being allowed for the coat and colour. The legs, tail, and head should also be patched, with small even patches on the ears. A blaze is liked on the face, that is, a stripe of cream or red running down from the forehead to the nose. The eyes may be copper or deep orange.

The Tortoiseshell-and-White have much the same standard, with the addition of white in the coat.

The coat should be well patched, with the three colours, black, red, and cream, well distributed and broken. A blaze is preferred on the face. There should not be too much, or too little, white. The type is as for other long-hairs and because of the cross-breeding is usually very good. The eyes may be deep orange or copper. Faults are tabby markings and smudging of the colours.

It is exceedingly difficult to breed Tortoiseshells to order and they may appear in litters when least expected. As they are females, a stud of one of the colours in the coat could be tried, that is a Black or Cream. A Red Self could be used, but a Red Tabby should be avoided as this could mean the introduction of tabby markings difficult to breed out.

The kittens in the litters are usually mixed, and may include Red, Blue-Creams, Creams, Blacks, and maybe a Tortoiseshell, but they are all very attractive.

It was once considered impossible to breed the Tortoiseshell-and-White to order, although it appeared from time to time from chance matings. Comparatively recently a cat fancier realized that by using cats with two-coloured coats, eventually recognized as Bi-Colours, bred from Tortie and White mothers, Tortie-and-Whites could be produced in litters more or less as required, although not all the kittens would be of that colouring.

Grooming is important for both varieties. Powder should be used sparingly as it dulls the colours.

Long-hair Tortoiseshell

Bi-Coloured Long-hairs

Cats with two-coloured coats have been known since the early days of the Cat Fancy, the black-and-white ones being referred to as 'Magpies'. They were exhibited in the Any Other Colour class, and although much admired, were usually sold as pets and neutered, being considered of little use for breeding. One fancier, interested in the breeding of Tortoiseshell-and-Whites, realized that using a Bi-Coloured produced by the correct breeding might produce kittens of the colours she was seeking to breed to order. This was most successful, and lead to the ultimate recognition of the Bi-

Colours. Unfortunately the standard that was granted was similar to that of the Dutch rabbit which has such an exacting pattern of markings that it proved impossible to breed in cats. Judges at the shows usually withheld the challenge certificates, with the result there were few champions. In 1971 the standard was revised allowing more flexibility in the distribution of the colour and white. The revised standard allowed not more than two thirds of the cat's coat to be coloured and not more than half to be white. Any solid colour is allowed. The face should be patched with colour and white. The eyes may be deep orange or copper in colour. Faults are tabby markings, long tails, and yellow or green eyes. The type is usually very good, probably because of the carefully selected breeding.

They are big cats and, probably because of this, the females kitten easily, producing progeny of various colourings, depending on the stud used. The litters should include Bi-Colours and there may also be some Self-coloured, and possibly Tortoiseshells. Whatever the colours, the kittens are most attractive, sturdy, and full of life.

Blue Creams

A very popular variety that arose by accident in the early days of cat breeding, but which was not recognized in Britain until 1929. They were known as 'Blue and Cream Mixed', also as 'Blue Tortoiseshell', but were also referred to as 'Oddities', as they were always female and very little was understood about breeding in those days.

At first the coats were patched and selective breeding was necessary to produce fur in the two colours of blue and cream intermingled. The standard in North America is still for patched coats.

The type is as for other long-hairs and is frequently outstanding, being bred by crossing Blues and Creams. The standard is for a dense, soft, and silky coat to consist of blue and cream softly intermingled. The large round eyes may be deep copper or orange in colour.

As the Blue Creams are a female-only variety, any males born invariably proving sterile, a Blue or a Cream stud should be used for breeding.

Faults are solid-blue or cream patches, although a cream blaze on the face is liked, and there should be no redness in the coat.

It is also possible for Blue Creams to appear in litters from Tortoiseshells.

Any Other Colour

This is a classification that is used for cats that conform to no recognized standard. They are often the result of experimental breeding when fanciers are endeavouring to produce a new variety, as was the case when Colourpoints were first bred, or may be the results of mismating, or some new mutation or variation in colour. Three generations of pure breeding are necessary before any new variety can be considered for recognition. This heading enables cats to be registered and also to be exhibited at shows in classes specifically for them. Such cats are not of course eligible for challenge certificates and cannot be champions.

Colourpoints (*Known as Himalayans in North America*)

The Colourpoints are an excellent example of a man-made variety produced by cross-breeding. To produce a cat with long-haired type and the Siamese coat pattern, that is, cream body colouring and dark points, took many years of selective breeding.

It was also difficult to get the bright-blue eye colouring of the Siamese in the large round eyes of the long-hairs, but this was done,

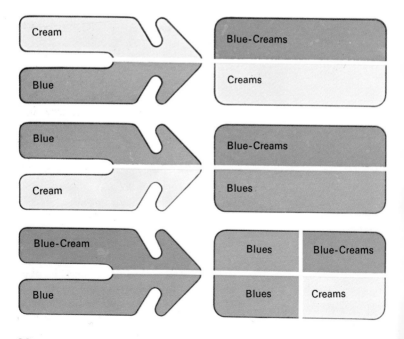

although sometimes the colour could still be a deeper blue. The standard calls for the fur to be long and thick with the pale body colouring in keeping with that of the contrasting points. The type should be as for other long-hairs and any similarity in type to the Siamese is a definite fault. Since 1955, when the Colourpoints were first recognized, they have become a very popular variety. They are now bred with seal points, Blue points, Chocolate points, Lilac points, Red points, and Tortie points, the last named being females only.

The kittens are born almost white with the contrasting point colouring appearing as the fur grows and it may be difficult sometimes to know what the ultimate colour will be. The kittens are always enchanting and attract much attention at the shows.

Birmans

A most distinctive variety with the coat pattern of the Colourpoints, but having the added attraction of four white paws. The white on the front feet should just cover the paws, while on the rear it should cover the paws and go up the back of the legs ending in a point like a gauntlet.

According to legend they are the descendants of the cats which were guardians of the temple in Burma, and for this reason they are also referred to as the Sacred Cats of Burma. More prosaically they are said to have originated in France in the 1920s from cross-breeding between the Siamese and long-hairs. They were recognized there in 1925 but it was many years before they appeared in Britain. First seen in the Any Other Colour classes they were granted championship status in 1966. Since then the variety has made great strides and has been exported all over the world.

The type is more like that of the original Angoras, the noses being a little longer and the ears taller. The fur is not so profuse and the tail is longer. The eyes should be a bright blue. The coat colour should be a golden beige, with contrasting points, which may be seal, blue, chocolate, or lilac.

The kittens are pale when first born, with the contrasting points appearing as the fur grows.

Turkish Cats

Another variety even closer in type and characteristics to the Angoras, the Turkish cats have been known in the Van area of Turkey for centuries. They breed true but because of the quarantine period imposed on cats coming from abroad it took a very long time to bring sufficient cats from Turkey to carry out the necessary breeding programme.

The standard calls for the long silky fur to be chalk white in colour, with auburn markings on the face; the ears to be white and the nose tip, paw pads, and inside the ears a delicate shell pink. The head is wedge-shaped and the ears should be large and upright, while the eyes should be light amber and pink-rimmed. The body should be long on sturdy medium-length legs, and the full tail should be longish rather than short, having faint auburn rings.

In Turkey they are reputed to like swimming in warm pools and shallow rivers, which may appear surprising, as it is frequently said that all cats dislike water. This, however, is not strictly true, as most like to play with water, and will swim if they have to, although not always willingly.

The fur is not as luxurious as that of most long-hairs. It grows quite thick in the winter with much of it being shed in the spring. The kittens are delightful in appearance, as even when newly born, the auburn markings show up clearly in the white fur.

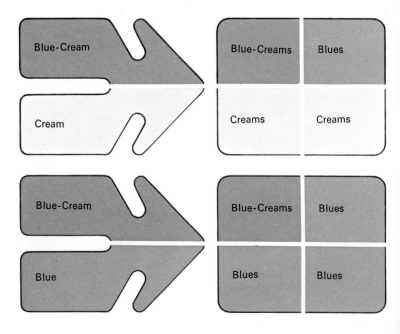

Colour points

Other Long-haired Varieties

Brief mention must be made here to other cats with long coats which are not recognized by the Cat Fancy in Britain.

Cameos: These are very striking cats which are being bred in small numbers in England, but are becoming increasingly popular in North America and Europe. There are a number of possible colour variations which include the Shell Cameo which resembles the Chinchillas, but the white fur is delicately tipped with red; the Shaded Cameo, with definite red shadings on the white coat; the Cameo Smoke or Red Smoke with undercoat of white and red contrasts; Cameo Tabby with pale-cream coat broken with well-defined red or beige markings. The type, which is very good, is as for other long-hairs.

Shaded Silver (*see Chinchillas*)*:* These are very close to the Chinchillas but the shadings on the white fur should be pure, unmarked silver; the whole effect being much darker than a chinchilla.

Blue Tabby and Cream Tabby: These are known in North America and have pale ground fur, one with blue tabby markings and the other with buff or cream markings.

Peke-Faced: Very similar in the general characteristics and colourings required for the Red Self and Red Tabbies but having a very short nose and type resembling that of the Pekinese dog.

Balinese: Known in the United States but not seen in Britain, these cats have Siamese type and coat pattern but long coats.

Maine Coon: An all-American cat, massive in size, said to have been produced originally by cross-matings of the resident domestic cats with those that arrived on ships from Russia and Asia long ago.

The heads are of medium width, with large pointed ears, big round eyes, and medium-length noses. The bodies are long, on tall legs, with long, full tails. Any colour or coat pattern is allowed.

Before the first official cat show was held in the United States, special shows were held for the Maine Coons.

Chocolate and Lilac Selfs: Two varieties now being developed in Britain are cats with coats the colour of milk chocolate and true lilac. The fur should be long and flowing and the type and characteristics are as for other long-hairs. A number of breeders are interested in these varieties, and it is probable that they will be recognized in the very near future.

Long-hair Birman

The Short-hairs

Short-haired cats fall into two main categories, 'Foreign' or 'Oriental', and 'British' or 'American'.

'British' cats all conform to a general standard which calls for cobby body structure, short, thick tails, broad heads with large round eyes and small ears. The legs should be short and sturdy and the overall effect should be one of compact strength and grace. The varieties differ basically only in coat colour and pattern. The fur should be short, fine, and close, never too fluffy.

In North America, in addition to the short-hairs already mentioned, there are the 'Exotics'. They have type similar to that of the long-hairs, with broad heads, short broad noses, full checks, small rounded ears and big round eyes. The colours recognized are as for most long-hairs, and an occasional out-cross with a long-hair is usually necessary to keep the type.

The American short-hairs have evolved from the original cats which are thought to have arrived with the Pilgrim Fathers. They are very like the British short-hairs, but the noses are slightly longer and the fur has not such a plushy appearance. The colours recognized are similar.

'Foreign' cats are completely different having long, lithe bodies, long heads, legs, and tails. Type varies slightly among the different varieties and from country to country. New breeds are being developed constantly. All short-haired cats are easy to maintain in good condition and with the minimum of grooming.

British Short-haired Breeds

White: British White cats are separated into two varieties, the Blue-eyed and the Orange-eyed; Odd-eyed whites are also known but are not eligible for championships in Great Britain. The standard for all is the same and calls for a pure-white coat with no dis-coloured hairs. Kittens occasionally have a few black hairs on their heads but these disappear as they grow older. These kittens are unlikely to be deaf as sometimes happens in the blue-eyed variety only.

Black: Usually of extremely good 'British' type, the black short-hair has a jet coat, sound to the roots and no trace of white hairs. The eyes are truly wonderful, being large, round, and well opened, and of a deep copper or orange colour.

Short-hair Blue

Short-hair Black

Blue: The most popular of the British breeds, the Blue short-hair, is an even blue all over, with no white hairs. Very affectionate, the Blue is extremely attractive with large, full, copper, orange, or yellow eyes.

Cream: Rich Cornish cream in colour, this variety is becoming increasingly popular. Tabby markings and bars are considered faults, the colouring being level and with no white hairs. Eye colour can be either copper or hazel.

Blue-Cream: Always female and the female equivalent of the Cream male (although female Creams are common too) due to the sex-linkage factor, these attractive cats have softly intermingled coats of pale-blue and cream hairs. In the U.S.A. the standard calls for the blue and cream areas to be in well-defined patches. Eyes may be copper, hazel, or yellow, but green is considered a fault.

Silver Tabby: Very difficult to breed to standard, the Silver Tabby has a body of pure silver with distinct black markings to an exactly defined pattern. The banding on the tail and legs must be evenly distributed and the black areas must not diffuse into the ground colour. With green or hazel eyes, a good Silver Tabby is a most eye-catching cat.

Red Tabby: Even more difficult to breed to standard than the Silver, the pedigree Red Tabby with the correct red ground colour and deeper brick-red markings is far removed from the many sandy and marmalade cats that can be seen. White, on the chest or tail tip, is considered a serious fault, and the markings must conform to the classic marbled pattern. Red Tabbies may have hazel or orange eye-colour.

Brown Tabby: The same classic pattern is called for on the Brown Tabby and must be carried through in dense black on a warm fawn background. There must be no trace of brindling or white markings and a white chin is a serious fault. Rarely seen at shows in recent years, a good Brown Tabby with orange, hazel, deep yellow, or green eyes will often take top awards.

Tortoiseshell: Usually female, the Tortoiseshell is due to the sex-linked red factor, and is the female equivalent of the Self-Red or Red Tabby, although females of those varieties also appear.

Short-hair Tabby

Exceptionally beautiful, the pedigree Tortoiseshell has a boldly patched coat of black, dark and light red, evenly distributed over the whole of the body, face, legs, feet, and tail. Each patch must be distinct and there must be no trace of white hairs. With eyes of copper, orange, or hazel, this variety is striking, especially when the desired, but not essential, red blaze is in evidence.

Short-hair Bi-colour

Tortoiseshell-and-White: As with the Tortoiseshell, female only; patches of red and black are called for in addition to white. The colours must be evenly distributed and the white should not predominate. With orange, copper, or hazel eyes and a white blaze, this is one of the most striking of short-haired breeds.

Spotted: Known for over a century, the Spotteds have made a comeback on the show bench recently. They may be of any colour, with the ground colour suitable to that of the spotting. The eye colour must also conform; for example, a silver spotted must have a background of pure silver, the spots being densely black, and the eyes green or hazel as in the classic Silver Tabby. The most show points are awarded for the spotting, which must be clearly defined and entirely separate. There must be no stripes, except on the head, and definitely no brindling.

Bi-Coloured: Exhibited for many years as Any Other Variety, the Bi-Coloured Short-hair is now recognized for championship status by the G.C.C.F. With a very exacting standard calling for markings which closely resembled those of a Dutch rabbit, good specimens were very hard to breed, but this standard has now been amended, as in the long-hairs. They may be Black-and-white, blue-and-white, orange-and-white, or cream-and-white with eyes of copper, orange, or amber.

Manx: A cat which stands in a class all its own is the Manx, which, although exhibiting most of the features of a typical short-hair, must be completely devoid of its tail, and have in its place a definite hollow. A characteristic rabbit-like hopping gait is another feature of this breed which has particularly long hind legs, and a rump said to be 'as round as an orange'. Manx cats can be of any pattern of colour but should have a double coat. True Manx cats are known as Rumpies while those offspring born with short tails are called Stumpies.

Foreign Short-hairs
Abyssinian: Of medium, foreign type with a heart-shaped face, the agouti Abyssinian with muddy brown fur ticked like a wild rabbit, is the perfect pet for the one-cat-only household. Known in Britain since 1880, the Abyssinian's nose leather and pads are black and eyes may be either green, yellow, or hazel.

Red Abyssinian: Identical to the normal Abyssinian except for the rich guinea-gold coat colour, and pink nose leather and pads which are attributed to a chocolate gene. These lovely cats turned up in occasional litters of normal Abyssinians until eventually they were developed as a separate colour variety and recognized as such by the G.C.C.F. in 1963.

Burmese: Burmese cats were first bred in the U.S.A. when a female kitten was brought from Burma in 1930. Eventually, when numbers increased and the breed became established, some Brown or Sable Burmese were sent to England to establish breeding strains, and from these beginnings the variety of Burmese seen on the show benches in England today first originated. Brown, Blue, and Cream Burmese are all eligible for championship status; also bred are Chocolate, Lilac, Red, and various Torties — Normal, Blue, Chocolate, and Lilac, some of which are very few in number and need carefully planned breeding programmes to improve type. The Brown Burmese has a very dark-brown coat and golden-yellow eyes, with less pronounced foreign type than the Siamese. The Blue Burmese is an antique-silver shade; the Cream is a delicate apricot; the Chocolate a pale milk chocolate with deeper points; the lilac a pale dove-grey; the red is a bright golden colour and the various Torties are of the four basic self shades mixed with red or cream. Faults in the Burmese which must be guarded against are green or torquoise eyes, white hairs, and tabby markings.

Havana: A man-made breed, the Havana is a self-chocolate Siamese with extreme foreign type. Mischievous and very affectionate, this mahogany-coloured cat with its brilliant lime-green eyes is often among the final line-up for top show honours throughout the world.

Rex (*Cornish*): Rex cats are the result of spontaneous mutations in various parts of the world. The Cornish ancestor appeared in an otherwise normal litter on a farm in Bodmin Moor, Cornwall, in 1950. Allowed in any normal coat colouration, the Cornish Rex must have a medium wedge-shaped head and large, round-tipped ears. The hard, muscular body, slender and *svelte,* must be well covered with short, thick, plush hair which must curl, wave, or ripple, and even the whiskers should be curly.

Rex (*Devon*): Due to a different gene from that which caused the

Cornish Rex to mutate, Devon Rex cats stem from Buckfastleigh Devon, and breeding programmes began in England in 1960. The pixie-like Devon Rex have full-cheeked faces with a distinct whisker-break, topped with large and wide-set ears. All colours are allowed with corresponding eye colour, and the short, fine coat is tightly waved.

Rex

Russian Blue: Russian Blue cats are highly intelligent, quieter than Siamese and differ from other Foreign short-hairs in having a double, sealskin-like coat, which is sound blue in colour, with a silvery sheen. The Russian with its vivid green eyes, is an easy and undemanding breed.

Breed Numbers

Short-haired Cats

14	White (Blue Eyes)	25b	Tailed Manx
14a	White (Orange Eyes)	26	Any Other Variety
14b	White (Odd Eyes)	27	Brown Burmese
15	Black	27a	Blue Burmese
16	Blue British	27b	Chocolate Burmese
16a	Blue Russian	27c	Lilac Burmese
17	Cream	27d	Red Burmese
18	Silver Tabby	27e	Tortie Burmese
19	Red Tabby	27f	Cream Burmese
20	Brown Tabby	27g	Blue-Cream Burmese
21	Tortoiseshell	28	Blue Cream
22	Tortoiseshell-and-White	29	Havana
23	Abyssinian	30	Spotted
23a	Red Abyssinian	31	Bi-Coloured
25	Manx	33	Cornish Rex
25a	Stumpiemanx	33a	Devon Rex

New Varieties

Foreign Lilac or Lavender: Known as Foreign Lilac in Britain, Short-hair in the U.S.A., and the Lavender in Europe, this unusual variety is a self-Lilac Siamese. With extremely foreign body lines, a delicate lavender coat and jewel-like green eyes, this rare cat is intelligent, super-affectionate, and quiet voiced.

Progressive breeders are always developing new varieties, and the 'self' equivalents of the Siamese make very attractive, aesthetically pleasing pets. Chocolate and Lilac have been standardized in self varieties and recognized in Britain, Europe, and the U.S.A. as Havana and Lavender or Foreign Lilac. Seal-point has been 'selfed' to give the Foreign Black or Ebony, and officially recognized in Europe, and breeders are developing 'selfed' tabby-pointed in various colours which are provisionally known as 'Egyptian Mau'.

Siamese

Siamese Cats, with their exotic colouring and blue eyes, were originally brought straight from the temples and palaces of Siam and efforts were made to procure more breeding pairs, from which the hundreds of Siamese kept today are descended. The range of colours that we now recognize is due to the manipulation by man of the cat's normal colour genes.

All Siamese, whatever their colour, are of the same type or conformation. The body is of medium size, long and, *svelte,* and the legs are long and slim, the hind-legs being longer than the forelegs. The feet are small and oval, and the tail long and whip-like. The head should be long and well proportioned with large wide-based and slightly pricked ears. The oriental eyes are always blue and slant towards the nose and must not show any trace of a squint. The colouring is apparent only on the points or extremities of the body — mask, ears, tail, legs, and feet; and the coat must be very short, fine in texture, glossy, and close-lying.

Siamese

Seal-pointed Siamese have cream bodies shading to warm fawn along the back and on the flanks. The points are a deep seal-brown, almost black, and the eyes are a clear deep and brilliant shade of blue. Prized attributes in the Seal-pointed are paleness of body colouring, and deep-blue eyes. This is the original colouration in the Siamese from which all other colour varieties have descended, and is affectionately known by fanciers as The Royal Cat of Siam.

The Blue-pointed Siamese were produced by the simple dilution of the black gene which produces the Seal-pointed. They are often slightly heavier in build than the Seal and are very attractive with white bodies shading to a slatey tone on the back and flanks. The points are a deep grey-blue and the eyes a clear and vivid bright blue. They are difficult to breed with the desired glacial coat colour, and consequently when good specimens do appear on the show bench they are hard to beat.

Chocolate-pointed Siamese also appeared naturally among the earlier Siamese and have made great strides in popularity in recent years due to their improvement in type and their retention of pale body colour throughout life. The body is a delicate ivory shade and the points are the colour of milk chocolate, a pleasing combination of coffee and cream. Eye colour is a clear, bright, vivid blue. The problems that beset breeders are those of producing matching points, as the forelegs of the Chocolate-pointed are often much paler than the ears and tail. This is a show fault.

When Siamese carrying both chocolate and blue genes were mated together, some very pale kittens appeared in the litters and puzzled breeders. It was then discovered that these ethereal little creatures which took so long to develop any points were in fact Lilac-pointed Siamese. These cats retain a pure-white coat through adulthood and have points of a delicate dove-grey. The eyes are the same as for Chocolate and Blue-pointed and the nose leather is violet. Called Frost-points in the U.S.A., when mated together, only lilac-pointed kittens can be produced.

Not being content with the four 'natural' varieties of Siamese, breeders, being ever progressive, decided to introduce other cat colours and patterns into the breed.

The Tabby-pointed is recognized in the four basic shades of Siamese, seal, blue, chocolate, and lilac, but the coloured points, instead of being solid, are broken into tabby stripes. The large ears have thumb-prints of colour on the backs and the tails are banded. Since their recognition the tabby-pointed, known as Lynx-points in other countries, have gained in popularity and rival the Seal-pointed for type and eye colour.

Red-pointed Siamese were originally bred when the red colour was introduced into a breeding programme by using a marmalade cat. Generations of careful matings have produced Siamese of outstanding type and completely Siamese features, but with beautiful white coats and points of bright reddish-gold. Combined with bright, vivid-blue eyes the effect in a good specimen is stunning. Faults include too much tabby marking on the face and tail and a diffusion of the apricot colouring into the body areas. Red is a sex-linked factor and so in the preliminary stages of breeding the Red-pointed Siamese, Tortoiseshell-pointed females were produced. These bizarrely-marked creatures were thought so attractive by breeders that they are recognized in their own right and may be produced in seal-tortie, blue-tortie (or blue-cream), chocolate-tortie, and lilac-tortie Siamese, and all are female only. The red factor when diluted, produces a very delicately marked Siamese known as the Cream-pointed or Ivory-pointed, which is white with the very palest apricot points and bright-blue eye colour.

Breed Numbers

Siamese

24	Seal-Pointed Siamese	32	Tabby-Point Siamese
24a	Blue-pointed Siamese	32a	Red-Point Siamese
24b	Chocolate-Pointed Siamese	32b	Tortie-Point Siamese
24c	Lilac-Pointed Siamese	32c	A.O.C. Siamese

Nutrition

Because cats are carnivores, many people feed their feline pets only muscle meat, often of the most expensive and best quality, taking care to remove all bone and fat, and cooking for long periods, mistakenly thinking that they are thus giving an ideal diet. Cats in the wild, however, catch rabbits, hares, birds, fish, and a variety of small rodents, occasionally supplementing their diet with grass-hoppers and insects. They eat the entire carcass, not merely the muscle of their prey and so ingest a quantity of partly digested vegetable matter from the entrails and the stomach. The wild cat kills every two or three days and gorges itself to the full eating very little the following day until hunger incites the hunting instinct once more. It is interesting to note that domestic cats have a tendency to follow this rhythmic feeding cycle when allowed to do so.

The main requirement in the cat's diet is water, which makes up 70 per cent of its body's composition, and it is essential that cats have access to fresh, clean drinking water at all times. Older cats in particular produce very small quantities of urine, which is highly concentrated, and inadequate water consumption is considered to be a prime factor in the formation of bladder stones in older cats, especially neutered males. Cats which do not appear to drink sufficient water should have a little common table salt sprinkled onto their meat meals. Cats which seem to drink excessively, however, may have kidney damage or diabetes, and the urine must be tested by the veterinary surgeon.

In addition to the water intake, five basic elements of nutrition are required by the cat each day: PROTEIN which is found in meat, eggs, cheese, and fish; CARBOHYDRATE found in sugars and starches; FAT from fat meat, butter, some fish, and cooking and other vegetable oils; VITAMINS and MINERALS found in various foods in a well-balanced diet. A high level of protein is required by the cat, therefore the bulk of all meals should consist of meat, with fish, eggs and cheese being given from time to time to vary the diet. The meat may be of any type including the better-quality canned varieties, but raw meat in lumps should be given occasion-ally to maintain healthy teeth and gums. Very little carbohydrate is needed by the cat and may be fed in biscuit form to bulk out meat meals, or in baby cereal or glucose added to milk. Cats need a high level of fat. A little ground fat meat is perfectly acceptable to most breeds, and a teaspoon of cooking oil or margarine may be added to lean-meat meals. The crisped fat from roast or grilled meat is a delicacy that some cats eat with relish. Fat is also obtained from milk and cream, but large pieces of suet-like fat should not be fed to cats as this may lead to vomiting. Of the cat's diet 20 – 25 per cent may consist of fat, but care should be taken not to include too much fish oil, which can cause disease. Minerals and trace elements are a tiny, but essential part of the cat's diet; they help in maintaining the delicately adjusted fluid balance in the body and also help to build bone. Domestic cats are often deficient in calcium, because most bones are removed from their meals. The deficiency is most apparent in kittens, and in lactating queens who deplete their entire skeletal reserve to make milk for their kittens. Kittens with calcium deficiency seem in normal health until they reach 15 or 16 weeks of age when they may become very quiet, nervous, and show signs of limping. X-Rays show greenstick fractures and severe skeletal defects. These are treated with large injections of calcium until the cats have recovered. It is extremely important to ensure that pregnant and lactating queens get enough calcium. If they are reluctant to drink milk, or milk upsets their digestion, calcium in tablet form must be given, as prescribed by the veterinary surgeon. The trace elements are required in minute amounts by the cat but are essential to good health. They include iron, copper, manganese, iodine, zinc, cobalt, and magnesium. Cats deficient in these have a very poor recovery rate after illness and little resistance to infection. Deficient kittens do not grow properly and have sparse coats, they do not play much but are gentle and loving. Home treatment must not be undertaken, however, as excessive amounts of trace elements can be as damaging as too little.

Vitamins are very complex substances which cannot be manufactured within the cat's body, so must be taken in as food. Many cats exhibit a deficiency of Vitamin A which can be overcome by feeding liver two or three times a week. In severe cases the veterinary surgeon will give the vitamin by injection. Cats deficient in Vitamin A have breeding problems and their muscles waste. The coat is sparse and the eyes look sore with conjunctivitis accompanied by a red-coloured discharge from the eye. If not checked, the eyes undergo changes and sight begins to fail. Deafness may also set in and in kittens signs of spasticity, especially in the hind limbs, becomes apparent.

The B group of vitamins are also important in the cat's diet but these may be destroyed during the processing of certain foodstuffs, so may be added to the meals in the form of Vitamin B-complex tablets. A cat deficient in Vitamin B^1 or Thiamin quickly loses appetite and weight, and becomes hypersensitive to touch. It develops neuritis with pain in the legs and the heart weakens. Deficiency in Vitamin B^6 or Pyridoxine leads to anaemia and kidney disease.

It may be seen, therefore, that the cat should be given a varied and well-balanced diet throughout life, one or two meals per day for adult cats, totalling 6 – 8 oz. of good-quality canned, dried, cooked, or raw meat, occasionally replaced by fish, eggs, or cheese. Raw liver two days each week and a milky drink at bedtime. Extra vitamins can be added to the diet from time to time to ensure that the level in the system is kept up. Kittens, pregnant and lactating queens, male cats used for stud purposes, and cats recovering from illness need more food and may have different nutritional requirements. Advice on correcting various deficiencies can be obtained from the veterinary surgeon, who can also dispense vitamin and mineral supplements of correct dosage.

Grooming

All cats should receive regular grooming sessions. The amount of effort required ranges from a perfunctory comb through every day for the short-haired house pet, to the sometimes twice-daily thorough brushing of the long-haired show champion. General care and maintenance also comes under the heading of 'grooming' and is virtually the same for all cats and kittens. Eyes and ears must be checked regularly, and wiped with dampened cotton-wool swabs whenever necessary. Any discharge from the eyes should be checked by the veterinary surgeon, as this can be the first sign of respiratory infection. Any unusual appearance of ear cavity must also receive professional attention to ensure that the troublesome earmites which cause 'canker' are not present. Kittens' ears do get grubby, but this easily wipes away, whereas in the case of canker, dark gritty flecks are seen in the entrance to the ear canal each day (*see Parasites*).

Claws also need regular inspection and if broken, or too long they may be trimmed back with nail clippers. Snip the ends straight across taking care to avoid the quick, as this may cause bleeding. Scissors must never be used for claw trimming, as these may splinter the claw and could cause lameness or an infected pad. As cats are so quick of movement and may be difficult to hold, it may be advisable to get a veterinary surgeon to clip the nails.

Short-haired cats are easy to groom and should be combed with a fine-toothed comb every day, from the head down to the tip of the tail to remove any dead or loose hairs. The coats can then be buffed up with a dry, soft chamois leather, or a silk scarf kept for the purpose. This makes the coat sparkle and keeps the muscles well toned. Hand-grooming firmly, and from head to tail with clean, dry hands has the same result and is much appreciated by most cats.

Long-haired cats need brushing right through every day, sometimes twice a day during the spring moult, or if they are to be entered for a show. Special attention must be paid to the fur under the body and any mats must be gently teased out with a coarse steel comb. The coat is then brushed through from tail to head, the frill is brushed up around the face, and the tail shaken gently by the tip to fluff it out. Light-coloured cats, both long-haired and short-haired, may have fine talcum powder sprinkled in the coat, rubbed well in and left for a few moments before being thoroughly brushed out. This cleans and separates the hairs and helps to prevent matting in the long-haired breeds. For dark-coloured cats, a silk

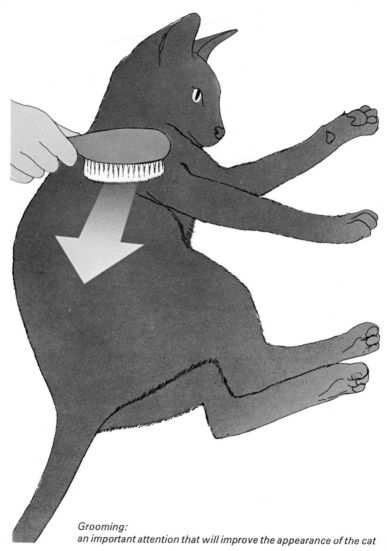

Grooming:
an important attention that will improve the appearance of the cat

scarf wrapped around the bristles of the brush helps to impart an extra sheen for show purposes.

The presentation and grooming of any cat for exhibition must be thorough and it is always advisable for the novice to be given a demonstration by an experienced breeder and exhibitor of the particular breed. Trimming, plucking, or shaping of the coat of any cat leads to disqualification from the show, and the same applies to any tinting, dyeing, or other artificial method of beautification. Any powder used for grooming must be completely brushed out of the coat before judging commences as the presence of any substance in the coat is an offence which could lead to disqualification.

Grooming is performed to remove all dead and unwanted hair from the coat, to clean the hair right down to the roots, to remove dead flakes of skin and dust or dirt which may have penetrated the coat, and to stimulate the circulation of the blood through the skin, promoting healthy new growth of hair from the follicles. It also tones up the muscles and gives the cat a feeling of warmth and well-being.

Cats which become very soiled, for example having explored the chimney, or the coal-hole, may be bathed, as this is virtually the only way to remove soot, coal-dust, or any other greasy substances from the cat's coat. It is usually necessary to have two people to bath a cat, one to hold on to him and the other to do the washing. The sink should have about six inches of warm water run into it, and a bucket of water at the same temperature placed on the draining board, with a large warm towel at the ready. The cat is placed gently in the sink and held by the assistant by the scruff. Water is scooped up and ladled all over the cat until the fur is saturated, which takes some time, for at first the fur repels the water. The head should not be wetted. The water is then let out of the sink and a mild, unscented shampoo is worked quickly and thoroughly into the coat and under the body. The rinsing water is then ladled from the bucket over the cat until all traces of shampoo are removed, then the surplus is pressed and squeezed from the fur. The cat is then wrapped carefully in the warm towel and the face can be washed with plain water and cotton wool. After a brisk rub with the towel, the cat should be put into a mesh or wicker carrier near some heat source or in the linen cupboard, in order to dry off thoroughly without delay. When dry the coat must be carefully groomed through.

Stud males and some breeding queens occasionally develop a

condition known colloquially as 'stud-tail' which is due to an accumulation of grease in the pores around the site of an active sebaceous gland near the root of the tail. To prevent the clogging of these pores and the subsequent abscess formation, this area should be checked frequently and any sign of grease dealt with at once. The area can be combed free of grease and then dusted with a little mildly antiseptic talcum powder. If the grease is persistent, or a thick layer builds up, then the area should be washed carefully with a good coal-tar soap, rinsed off thoroughly, as coal-tar derivatives are toxic to cats, and carefully dried. If neglected, and an abscess forms, protracted antibiotic treatment may be necessary to clear it up. Another gland which occasionally causes trouble, particularly in red cats, is sited in the chin, and when over-active or damaged by a hard knock, perhaps by jumping badly, a clear liquid is exuded from the pores which dries to form black spots under the chin and along the edges of the lips. Again, gentle washing and drying, and the application of a mildly antiseptic talcum powder will effect a rapid cure.

Reproduction

Unlike the dog which has two well-regulated periods of heat each year, the female domestic cat, if not impregnated, will continue a frequent oestral cycle. Mature, entire males will mate at all periods of the year, although cats leading a life of complete freedom do tend to have periods of sexual quiescence during the coldest months of the year. Sexual maturity in the male is attained between 6 and 18 months and 4 to 12 months in the female. The Foreign Short-haired breeds mature earlier on average than the Persians, and Siamese are particularly precocious. Females born early in the year appear to have their first season very early the following spring, while those born in late summer or autumn usually come into heat in the late spring of the following year. Mild weather following cold spells seems to induce oestrus in female cats, so this would indicate that climate plays an important part in the breeding cycle.

Male cats do not have periods of 'heat' and are capable of coition at any time after reaching sexual maturity, being stimulated by the scent of a queen in season. Female cats 'call' for a mate. The call varies from gentle cries in the short-haired house pet to banshee wails from the safely confined Siamese. The dreadful wailing of cats on the rooftops is made by several tom-cats in the vicinity of a queen on heat. They congregate and square up to one another trying to determine which one shall be first to mate with her. Fighting, when it breaks out, is fierce and takes place in silence, while the queen rolls and poses, until mated by the strongest male. Other males will also mate her in fairly quick succession and her resulting litter could be sired by two or three different cats. As well as becoming pregnant, the queen may pick up all manner of parasites and infections and may become bitten or scratched with resulting abscesses. All this requires expensive treatment, so it breeding is the aim, controlled matings are essential.

A pedigree stud male lives off the fat of the land. He is dearly loved and prized by his owner and housed in his own specially designed stud accommodation. In temperate climates, stud males are usually kept outside. The stud has a large cedar-wood shed, smoothly lined and painted inside for easy cleaning. The floor is usually tiled or covered with washable vinyl or linoleum, and the cat is provided with heating and lighting, comfortable bedding, exercise shelves, and a special pen for his visiting wives. A large paved or concreted run, safely wired in, complete with tree trunks to strop surrounds his stud house, and he is kept fit and well fed,

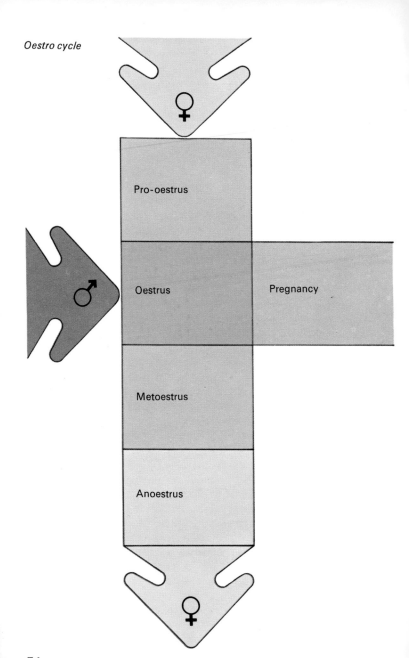

Oestro cycle

Pro-oestrus

Oestrus

Pregnancy

Metoestrus

Anoestrus

54

possibly making occasional sorties to cat shows to pick up a few more ribbons. Owners of suitable pedigree queens can book service by the male and when they show signs of heat, their owner telephones the stud owner and arranges a suitable time to arrive with the queen, who will be left 'at stud' for two to six days.

Pedigree female cats are usually allowed to mate on their second heat, if they have grown to full size, and are generally sound and healthy. The first stage of the heat is known as the pro-oestrus period, during which the uterus and vagina prepare for copulation and possible pregnancy, the cat's appetite increases, and she becomes ultra-affectionate and very restless. The second stage develops about four to five days after the onset of pro-oestrus, and is the true period of oestrus when mating and conception can occur. This lasts for four to seven days. During this time the queen rolls on the floor, postures, and cries. In some breeds, notably the Siamese varieties, these cries reach an alarming pitch. The cat may not eat at all during this period and will make repeated attempts to get out of the house to find a mate. If mating is withheld, no ova are released, for in the cat ovulation only occurs after coition, and a third stage called metoestrus is entered during which the reproductive organs settle down into the fourth, a resting stage — anoestrus — before the next cycle begins again.

If mating takes place successfully, and ovulation occurs normally, the kittens are born approximately nine weeks later, gestation being in the region of sixty-five days duration. The average litter size is three to five kittens. The male cat plays no part whatsoever in the life of the pregnant or nursing queen. In the wild the male may harm the kittens should he find them, and female cats, even in the safety of a modern home, tend to try to hide away their litter for the first few weeks of their lives.

Pregnant queens live normally for the first three weeks after conception, then the nipples may enlarge and look pink, and a slight thickening of the body takes place. An increase in the appetite is noticed and the cat seems settled and contented. Extra milk or calcium should be given and she should be checked for internal and external parasites before the kittens are born. About thirty-five to forty days after mating the abdomen is quite swollen and she will roll on the ground when she feels the kittens' movements inside her. Two or three days before the birth she will start restlessly looking for a suitable 'nest' and should be provided with a large box of newspapers in a dark, warm, and quiet spot. The shape of the abdomen changes just before the birth and she

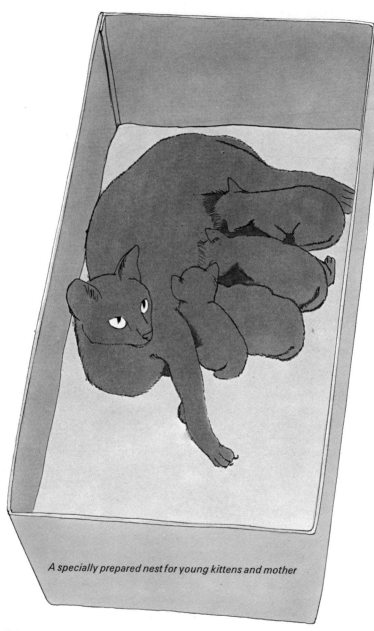

A specially prepared nest for young kittens and mother

will become more pear-shaped as the kittens move towards the birth canal, and milk will form in the breast.

After tearing up newspapers she will settle when her true labour begins and will probably cope quite adequately with the kittens as they are born, but she may need help, so should not be left unattended, especially with her first litter. The contractions start and become steadily stronger until a bubble appears from the vagina. This is a membrane filled with fluid which clears the birth canal. She will lick and pull this away with her teeth. The kittens may be born head first or breech, either way is quite natural and each is enclosed in a membrane and attached by an umbilical cord·to a placenta. The queen licks the membrane from the kitten and severs the cord, her rough tongue stimulating the kitten to gulp in his first breaths of air. The placenta is passed next and usually eaten by the queen, helping to stimulate the milk flow in her own body. She should be allowed to cope alone unless she neglects to clear the mucus from the kitten's mouth and nose. The other kittens should follow at intervals after the first, and the time taken for the whole delivery can vary from two or three hours to two days without distress to the queen. If strong contractions go on for two hours or so without any sign of a kitten, the veterinary surgeon should be called in, having been asked to stand by beforehand.

When the queen has had her final kitten she will gather them all to her and this is the time to offer an egg beaten with evaporated milk and a tablespoon of boiling water and two teaspoons of glucose. A fresh pad of newspapers with a clean blanket and piece of boiled sheet wrapped around them should be warmed, and the litter placed carefully on it. All the soiled paper should be removed and the fresh bedding and kittens carefully placed to allow the queen to rest. The cords should be checked and if really necessary may be trimmed back to about one inch with sterilized scissors. The end of the cord should be dabbed with an astringent solution obtained from the veterinary surgeon to prevent any infection entering.

Having cleaned up after the birth and consumed the rich placentas, and gratefully eaten the egg and milk, the queen may remain with her kittens several hours. Fresh water and a toilet tray should be provided, and if she has not used the latter within twenty-four hours she should be encouraged to do so. While lactating the cat should be given as much food as she wants. Some cats will decide to wean their kittens by offering them bits of meat at about four weeks. About this time they may be given a little baby food or alternatively tinned milk, specially prepared milk powder, finely minced meat, a little mashed fish, or baby cereal. They will eat more and more and take less milk from their mother until at eight weeks they may be separated from her entirely, although they should not go to new homes until they are at least ten weeks of age.

If necessary the kittens should be wormed under veterinary advice at about seven weeks of age. They should also be checked over to make sure they are growing well and have correct dentition. The veterinary surgeon's advice as to vaccination against Feline Infectious Enteritis should be followed, and the kittens treated accordingly. By this time they will be having five small meals per day and using their toilet tray. They will play happily together and with toys and providing they have received lots of loving care and handling, will have developed perfect temperaments and be ready to delight their new owners.

In the majority of cases parturition goes according to plan, but occasionally things go wrong and the queen's owner has to help out. Kittens may be born in such rapid succession that the female does not have the time or energy to clean them, or her labour might be so painful that she turns on her kittens and tries to kill them. In both instances, another box with a well-wrapped hot water bottle inside must be ready and the kittens taken up and wiped clean, paying particular attention to the nostrils and mouth. The cord is then cut with sterile scissors about one inch from the navel, and the end pinched between finger and thumb for thirty seconds to prevent blood loss. A dab of an astringent solution obtained from the veterinary surgeon will help, and also prevent infection entering the kitten's body through the cord. The kitten should then be placed on the left palm, head tilted downwards and rubbed briskly with a small piece of towelling to dry him and stimulate his heart and lungs into action. A piece of damp cotton-wool should be used to simulate the licking of the mother's tongue around the genital area. When the kitten appears to be breathing regularly, he should be placed in a warm box and the next one attended to in the same way. When all the kittens are born, the mother may accept and feed them normally, but if she still turns on them viciously they may have to be hand-reared.

Rearing your kitten

It is up to you to rear and train your kitten, and to develop his character. He should be provided with a toilet tray, such as a polythene washing-up bowl, which may be placed on a large sheet of newspaper in a convenient spot, and a quarter filled with cat-litter, torn tissue paper, or wood shavings. Show him this from time to time until he has once used it, then he will know exactly where he is expected to go in future. Always keep the litter changed as kittens will not use a damp or soiled tray, and do not move the tray from place to place, or he may get confused and use the floor where the tray had been placed previously.

A warm and draughtproof bed is essential and a small cardboard box packed with a thick layer of newspapers topped by a warm and easily laundered piece of blanket, or an old sweater is ideal. At first the kitten will miss his litter-mates, and the comfort of a well-wrapped hot-water bottle may be provided. Children must be taught to avoid picking up the kitten during his sleeping periods — he will play vigorously, then curl up to sleep several times each day, and it is important that these rest periods are respected. He must not be dropped, trodden on, or allowed to jump down from any height at this age, as irreparable injuries could be sustained. Electric flex presents another hazard to the young kitten during teething, when he will chew anything he can get his little jaws around, so all plugs should be withdrawn from their sockets when he is left unattended, or looped up out of his reach. Toys such as ping-pong balls, woolly animals, and pipe-cleaner spiders should be provided, and an empty paper bag for him to dive into will provide amusement for both the kitten and the family.

Diet is of prime importance, and the breeder's instructions must be followed to the letter for the first ten days, after which any adjustments must be made gradually. Four or five meals daily will suffice up to the age of six months, two daily meals from six to twelve months, then one main meal per day is quite adequate for neutered cats, although stud males and breeding queens should remain on two main meals daily during the breeding season. In addition to this, a nightcap should be given of diluted evaporated milk, perhaps reinforced with baby cereal or an egg, to which any recommended vitamin supplement can also be added.

Meals can consist of canned, cooked, or raw meat, cooked fish or rabbit, canned pilchards, mackerel or sardines, or the excellent complete dried cat diets. Fresh, clean drinking water must be available at all times. The quantities of the meals will obviously vary according to age and bodily requirements, but a good basic guide to total daily consumption is to allow $1\frac{1}{2}$ oz. of food for each 1 lb. of body weight up to one year of age, then 1 oz. of food per 1 lb. of body weight thereafter, although commonsense must prevail, for the metabolism of cats can vary as it does in humans, and some animals require more food than others. Cats should be well-muscled, but never allowed to become overweight, as this puts an unnecessary strain on the heart, and may shorten the cat's life.

The main rules for successful feeding are simple: always feed good-quality and varied meals at room temperature, and never offer anything even slightly tainted, or straight from the refrigerator. Uneaten food must be discarded, never kept back to be offered again later; milk and meat must not be fed together as this causes gastric upsets; small and splinterable bones must always be removed before feeding cooked meats.

Your kittens must be regularly groomed to keep their coats in good condition and their muscles well toned (*see Grooming*) and they should be neutered if you do not intend to breed cats in a serious and responsible way. The neutering of male cats is called castration, and of female cats, spaying, and both operations can be carried out from about four months onwards. Most veterinary surgeons advise the age of four to six months for either operation. If delayed until eight to ten months, especially in the case of the young male, when the adult musculature is laid down, a harder and leaner adult neutered cat is produced. It is often thought that a female should be allowed to have a litter before spaying, but this is not kind, and makes the spaying operation more serious.

In castration of the male kitten, the testicles are removed, and this has the effect of preventing the urine from developing its characteristic 'tom-cat' odour. The young castrated male will not roam the countryside looking for mates or picking fights with all other felines, and so will avoid the torn eyes and ears and the horrific abscesses which result from cat fights. Castration is a simple operation in young kittens and is always performed under anaesthetic; it becomes slightly more complex with increasing age: as the testicles increase in size, their blood supply also increases, and there is more risk of haemorrhage. No stitches are inserted, and your kitten, having been deprived of food for several hours before receiving the anaesthetic, is soon back at home demanding his supper. Spaying is the only really satisfactory way of preventing a female cat from having kittens, and is much kinder than allowing

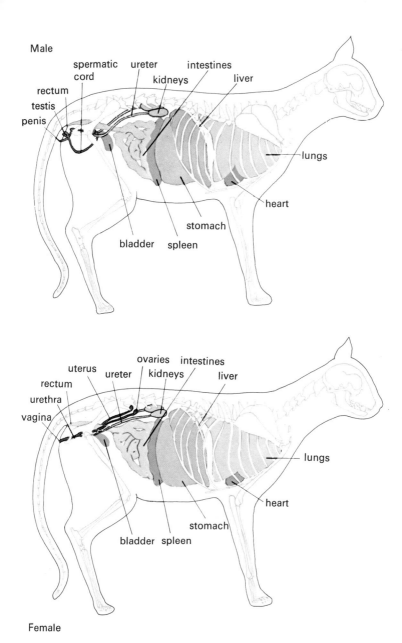

Male

spermatic cord
ureter
intestines
kidneys
liver
rectum
testis
penis
lungs
heart
stomach
bladder   spleen

ovaries
uterus
intestines
rectum
ureter
kidneys
liver
urethra
vagina
lungs
heart
stomach
bladder   spleen

Female

her to come into heat six times a year and trying to keep her safely indoors. The operation is best performed in kittenhood. With the cat anaesthetized, a small incision is made by the surgeon either through the flank or along the belly, and the uterus and ovaries are removed. Usually only a couple of stitches are necessary to close the incision, and these are removed after about ten days when the wound has healed. The kitten must be deprived of food for some hours before receiving the anaesthetic to prevent vomiting on the operating table, which can lead to choking and subsequent death. A longer period is spent under the anaesthetic, so the recovery time is a little longer for female cats, but after a night's rest and a good meal, she will be none the worse for the experience.

Your kitten may be trained to use the garden for toilet purposes if you wish, by showing him the spot you wish him to use whenever you notice him going to his tray, but he must be confined to the house at night for safety and should always have his toilet tray in situ. In these days of cat-napping for skins and research purposes, and fast-moving motor traffic, many cats are destined to live their entire lives indoors and do not seem to suffer any ill consequences. The Foreign Short-hair breeds including all the Siamese varieties, even seem to prefer this mode of life, and are therefore admirably suitable for flat-dwellers or those living near busy main roads. Cats kept entirely indoors in this manner should be provided with pots of cocksfoot grass to chew on when the mood takes them, and should

Litter tray

have their claws shortened with nail clippers, carefully avoiding the quick. Scratching posts are a must for claw stropping, or better still, a stout mat made of coconut matting tacked to a stout board. Kittens soon learn that this is the place to strop, and that the lounge suite is strictly taboo!

Indoor cats have the advantage of avoiding infestation by parasites such as worms, fleas, and ear-mites, but also avoid all low-grade infections and do not gain natural immunity to odd feline diseases, so may be more susceptible to infection when taken out of their home environment and subjected to exhibition at cat shows, or placed in boarding kennels for the holidays. It is up to every prospective cat-owner to decide at the outset whether his cat is to be given complete freedom or to live confined to the home or an enclosed pen. It would be extremely cruel to expect a formerly free-ranging cat to accept a life of confinement, and equally so for an indoor dweller to be turned loose into a strange environment.

Orphan Kittens: Orphaned or rejected kittens are best cared for by a foster mother. If a cat can be found with a small and newly-born litter, one or two kittens can be carefully introduced and she will accept them as her own offspring. The foster queen should be taken from her nest to feed and while she is away, the orphaned kittens should be gently rubbed all over with the hind parts of the queen's own kittens in order to make them smell right, then tucked up in the nest along with the others. When the queen returns to the nest, she will not be completely fooled by the newcomers, but after a good lick all over, she should settle down to nurse them along with her own.

If a foster mother is not available, the kittens may be reared by hand, but this is a long and tedious business and great thought must be given to embarking upon it for it is easier to have new-born kittens put to sleep by the veterinary surgeon than to be forced by fatigue to take them along two weeks later. The queen spends most of her time caring for her babies, cleaning them, feeding them and keeping them at a constant temperature, and the human foster parent must be prepared for a lot of work to compensate for the loss of the kittens' natural mother.

The first essential is the constant temperature: a thermometer should be fixed in the box near the kittens, who need about 32 °C. for the first twenty-four hours of life, 29 °C. for the next week, 27 °C. for the following week, and then 21 – 24 °C. The temperature should be carefully checked and kept as even as possible. Heat is best provided by the suspension of an infra-red bulb over the box, the height of the cord or chain being shortened or lengthened until the correct temperature at kitten level is achieved. In an emergency an ordinary electric light bulb may be used, but the kittens may find this disturbing as their eyes begin to open, at four to twelve days, and until the eyes are fully open they should not be subjected to strong day or artificial light.

Inside the box should be placed several layers of paper towelling, the top layers can be shredded for comfort, and as this becomes soiled, the soiled area can be removed. Other equipment needed is a stock of 5 ml. disposable syringes, some valve rubber from the bicycle repair shop, snd some scales. If the kittens disturb or try to suckle one another, a set of small boxes can be placed inside the large box and each lined with paper towelling, to form individual beds for the kittens. The kittens should each be weighed and the weight recorded daily, showing a steady gain. The best formula for feeding is to use the specially prepared powdered-milk supplements, which must be reconstituted according to instructions. Undiluted evaporated milk warmed to blood heat is excellent; cow's milk with a little glucose and an egg yolk added can be used in an emergency. To feed the orphans, first wash the syringes and valve rubber which should be cut into lengths of about 2 cm. These short pieces are then fitted carefully onto the ends of the syringes for the kittens to suck. The syringes are filled with the warm milk mixture and the kittens will usually suck happily at the 'teats'. Great care must be exercised in depressing the syringe plunger so that the kitten is not choked, for if any liquid is ingested into the lungs, pneumonia will set in and the kitten will die. Each kitten should take about 5 ml. of milk every two hours for the first twenty-four hours, and then may well accept one and a half syringes at each meal. Feeding techniques are developed by practice, but it is best to start with the kittens comfortably on a warm towel on one's lap as the feeding takes some time. The filled syringes should be kept in a jug of hot water to keep them at a constant temperature until required; each kitten should have its own syringe so that it gets the correct amount of milk. The two-hourly feeding should be carried out for the first three days at least, longer if possible, but may then be reduced to three-hourly sessions. Night feeding can be discontinued after the first week, feeding at midnight, then leaving the kittens until seven or eight o'clock in the morning.

As important as the feeding is the stimulation that makes the kittens urinate and empty their bowels. After the kittens have been bottle fed, they should be turned gently on their backs, and the mother's washing action should be simulated by gently wiping the genital region with cotton-wool wrung out in warm water, until the kitten urinates. Often solid motions will be passed also, although these may be without stimulation at other times. The kittens should also be kept clean around the mouth and chin, and the eyes should be bathed daily once they open. Talcum powder can be used on the kittens to help keep them clean and dry, and a little petroleum jelly can be used for any soreness of the hind region. Hand-reared kittens should be taught to lap as early as possible, certainly by four weeks of age, and should be eating creamed fish, and other easily mashed foods at the earliest possible moment. Cereals are not recommended as the kitten needs to consume large quantities in order to get enough protein, and tiny kittens very quickly tire of eating. Chopped hard-boiled eggs are excellent, and meat stewed in bone stock, minced, returned to its stock, and reduced for two or three hours, cools to a thick and very nutritious jelly which the kittens cannot resist.

Toys: a diversion for any kitten

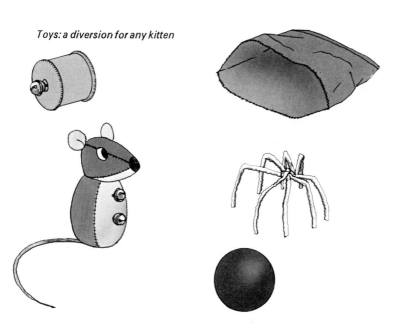

Hand-reared kittens each require 1,000 units of Vitamin A added to their diet each day which may be given in the form of cod-liver oil for convenience sake. The motions must be watched for signs of abnormality. The normal consistency is of thick cream and a cream-yellow or greyish colour, getting darker and slightly firmer as solids are introduced to the diet. Deviations from this pattern should be reported to the veterinary surgeon who will advise accordingly. The other problem with such kittens is that not having had the benefit of their mother's colostrum to give them immunity against disease, they are very susceptible to all manner of infections. They should not therefore be exposed to lots of admiring visitors or other animals, and a course of vaccination may begin much earlier than would be considered wise in a normal litter.

Accidents

Despite wonderfully fast reflexes and acute powers of hearing, sight, and smell, the cat is, nevertheless, prone to accidental injury both on the road and in and around the home and garden. Having very little road sense, cats should always be kept indoors at night, when the majority of feline road accidents occur, presumably when the cat's pupils are fully dilated for hunting at night and the sudden dazzling glare of headlights proves too confusing for the usual avoiding action to be taken. Most road accidents are fatal, but some merely stun the unfortunate animal, which may spend several days in a shocked condition in a ditch or hedgerow.

A cat which has been involved in a road accident should be lifted gently onto a coat or piece of board. A restraining hand on the scruff of the neck may be necessary if the animal is so badly injured that it tries to bite. It should be taken as quickly as possible to the nearest veterinary surgeon, always preferable to calling the veterinary surgeon to attend at the roadside. Should the cat be bleeding profusely, the wound should be bandaged firmly with a handkerchief or scarf until professional help is to hand. In many cases of road accident, the cat will sustain rupture of the diaphragm and crushing of the ribcage and it is important in these cases to place the cat's head higher than the rest of the body with the chin tilted slightly upwards to help the laboured breathing. If on the other hand there is bleeding from the mouth or throat, the head must be lowered slightly, so that blood does not flow back and into the lungs. An unconscious cat should have its mouth checked to ensure that the tongue is not blocking the airways.

Remarkably, cats often treat a serious road accident as just one of their nine lives, and broken legs, crushed ribs and fractured jaws mend rapidly. Even internal injuries are overcome in the majority of cases providing that veterinary help is not delayed.

A very common accident sustained by adventurous pets in the day and age of the apartment-dweller, is that caused by misjudged landings, such as from an upstairs balcony onto a concrete pathway at ground level. Kittens occasionally jump down from trees or walls, landing badly, tipping over from front paws onto the face, usually fracturing the palate and the fragile bone structure at the back of the nostrils and causing a very swollen face with much difficulty in eating and drinking for some weeks. Older cats when landing on the head often cleanly fracture the jawbone at its central junction, which needs to be carefully wired or pinned until completely healed. Veterinary treatment will mend these injuries in most cases, but the owner must persevere in getting the animal to take sufficient nourishing food to maintain bodily condition, and when eating is difficult and painful, hand-feeding with finely minced or creamed meals may be necessary. Cats are fastidious in their habits, but if too ill or injured to manage a sanitary tray, the bed must be lined with layers of crumpled toilet tissue, changed regularly throughout the day. The anal regions should be kept bathed, dried and lightly dusted with talcum powder.

Accidents to claws are quite common, sometimes the whole claw is pulled out and a severe swelling of the paw rapidly follows. After veterinary antibiotic treatment, it is often necessary to bathe the affected foot two or three times daily. Use water at room temperature with a little Epsom salts dissolved in it. The cat can be placed comfortably on a thick folded towel in his owner's lap and the solution, in a jam jar, is slipped up over the affected foot. Most cats immediately appreciate the warm relief afforded and settle down happily for five minutes or so, after which the paw can be carefully dried with cotton-wool. Claws are torn in climbing, getting caught in brickwork, tree bark, or, more seriously, in wire netting, when the cat may take his whole body weight on the trapped foot. As well as claw damage, there may be a temporary injury to the nerves of the leg with swelling or even paralysis for a while. Obviously, veterinary treatment is necessary for any injury of this nature.

Other accidents sustained by cats out of doors are usually caused by the cat's own curiosity, and include falling into swimming pools and being unable to climb out again; exhaustion and death by drowning eventually follow. Cats are often shot by accident while hunting rabbits, and occasionally are shot by design by trigger-happy young men with airguns. Luckily these pellets are rarely fatal, and usually easy to remove, and although causing pain, may not do any permanent damage.

A cat covered with paint, paraffin, or tar must be cleaned up without delay. Wipe off the substance with wads of rag or tissue, then apply any kind of fat — lard, margarine, cooking oil, or butter — rubbing it into the fur and wiping off as much as possible. Speed in working is vital as the cat's skin will absorb the substance and severe chemical burns will ensue. Wash the cat quickly, gently, and thoroughly with mild detergent, rinse with warm water and towel as dry as possible. Give the cat warm milk and glucose, and settle it in a warm dark place, such as a box in the airing cupboard, to recover

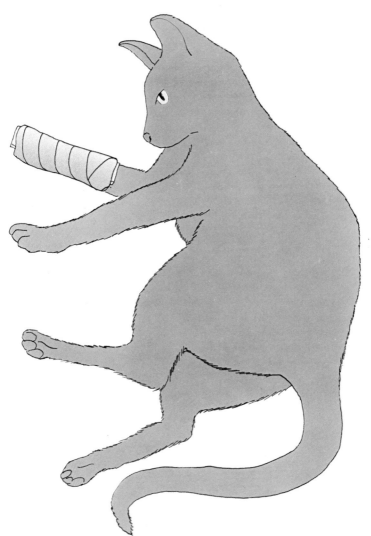

Prompt and careful treatment can save a cat much unnecessary pain

from the shock he has sustained. If the cat started licking himself clean before treatment, some medication is called for, to offset the highly toxic effects of the substance licked and ingested. Several weeks may elapse before the internal damage is repaired and the cat is restored to full health and normal appetite.

Bites from other cats, especially in the cases of troublesome males, can cause very nasty abscesses. The canine teeth cause deep punctures, usually in pairs, one by the upper and the other by the lower tooth. These marks are usually invisible on the surface under the fur and seal over quickly, leaving the bacteria introduced beneath the skin to multiply rapidly, forming the abscess within forty-eight hours. Some days may elapse before the owner notices anything amiss with his pet, by which time he is probably running a high temperature, and veterinary treatment is necessary to open and treat the abscessed area which must then be bathed and filled with antibiotic ointment until healed from the inside.

In the height of summer, cats may have trouble with grass seeds and barley awns, which can work into the eye behind the third eyelid, or down into the ear canal, and sometimes into the skin between the toes. Country-dwelling cats should be checked over at regular intervals to ensure that clinging seeds are not attached to any part of the coat. Prickly seed cases stick the hairs together in clumps and can cause severe matting of the coat, and if licked and swallowed during the cat's toilet, cause intestinal upset. Barley awns in the eyes must be removed very carefully so that the 'whiskers' do not get left behind. The cat should be held by an assistant and saline solution or even cold tea is trickled into the open eye when the awn should float out. If really embedded, awns have to be removed under anaesthetic by the veterinary surgeon.

Most common of feline accidents in the home are those of electric shock, when young kittens bite into live electric flexes. When appliances are in use, make sure that the flexes are tucked away neatly into the skirting board, or looped up out of the cat's way. Burns from hot fat are best avoided by removing cats from the kitchen while the dinner is cooking! Washing machines, spin and tumbler dryers, and refrigerators have all turned into coffins for cats, and the doors of such equipment should be kept closed, and if in use while the cat is around, a visual check should be carried out as routine before closing the door of any appliance.

Cats are notoriously fastidious about what they eat and therefore rarely get poisoned, although for some reason they seem to have a penchant for the taste of anti-freeze, which should be kept safely bottled and corked. Most cases of suspected poisoning in the cat turn out to be the onset of one of the serious virus diseases, and any cat showing symptoms of poisoning, such as vomiting, diarrhoea, unsteadiness, extreme lethargy, or collapse, should receive veterinary attention without delay. If your pet did die through 'poisoning', and did not have an autopsy performed, you should wait for three months before getting a replacement kitten, just in case it was Feline Infectious Enteritis.

Scratching at the mouth usually means that a fish bone has become lodged either across the palate or between the teeth. The cat must be wrapped in a towel and held by an assistant, while a teaspoon handle is used to prize out the bone. Small chop bones often get caught in the teeth and are difficult to free with the spoon handle. When this happens use the spoon to wedge the cat's mouth open while you work the bone free with your fingers. Bones in the throat must be removed professionally, and without delay.

After any accident, a cat must be treated for shock and needs warmth and rest. A warm blanket and perhaps a hot water bottle, well wrapped, placed in his travelling basket is ideal, then the cat can be warm and confined in a darkened room to recover. After a period of rest, warm milk and glucose may be offered but the cat must never be forced to drink at this time.

Prevention is always better than cure, and a knowledge of the hazards that your cat may face will help in taking preventive measures. Sharp-edged tin cans and bones should be placed in dustbins with well-fitting lids. In areas with busy roads, cats should be accustomed to a life indoors, or the garden should be fenced if possible. Paint, and other toxic substances, must have safely-fitting lids. The lavish use of pesticides and disinfectants can be fatal to the domestic cat, and regular checking of the skin, ears, mouth, and paws should be a routine habit, started during kittenhood.

Home nursing

When sick, a cat needs the same sort of care and attention as any other member of the family: warmth, nourishing light diet, cleanliness, and the comfort of loved ones close at hand.

Whether following a serious accident or virus infection, the same basic care is essential to effect a full recovery. The patient needs a warm draughtproof bed and ideally this should be a cardboard box of suitable size with layers of newspapers for bedding topped with a disposable paper towel which can be changed daily and burnt. This box should be placed in any warm spot, or have an infra-red heating bulb suspended over it. It should be away from noise and bustle, and preferably off the floor. The cat must be fed, and if very ill, this will have to be done forcibly, using a plastic syringe (with the needle removed) filled with liquid foods such as beaten egg, milk, and glucose, liquidized meat juices, or creamed soups. Liquids of a creamy consistency are easier for the cat to swallow than watery ones. The cat's head must be raised and the chin tilted upwards, the syringe is then inserted into the side of the mouth between the teeth, the mouth is kept closed and the handle gently depressed. Patience and practice are required to feed a sick cat successfully in this way, but it may well save his life. After feeding, bathe the mouth, and sponge off any spilled food. Fresh water should be readily available to the sick cat, should it decide to drink voluntarily, and when the appetite returns, strong-smelling food should be offered. Herrings, kippers, and pilchards are very useful and even fish paste can be used to get the cat back to normal eating habits.

Most sick animals need courses of antibiotic treatment, and these will be administered by the veterinary surgeon, at first by injection, but he may leave tablets or capsules to be given at prescribed intervals if the illness is prolonged. A whole tablet or capsule is given by placing the left hand over the cat's head and opening its mouth be gently pressing the cheeks on either side with thumb and forefinger. The pill is dropped at the back of the throat with the right hand, the mouth allowed to close, and the throat massaged until the pill is swallowed. After a severe respiratory illness, however, the soreness and ulceration of the mouth and throat may make such treatment difficult and the contents of the capsule can be emptied onto a saucer, or a tablet crushed with the back of a spoon. The powdered grains can then be pressed into a pea-sized knob of butter with a teaspoon handle until all the powder is absorbed, then the butter mixture slipped onto the back of the tongue. It is essential that the whole dose is taken by the cat, and if the medicine is very bitter, honey may be tried instead of butter. Liquid medicines can be given in the same way as liquid foods.

The third essential in successful home nursing of cats is that of cleanliness, for all cats abhor being dirty, and if so sick that they cannot clean themselves, this function must be carried out for them. With an incontinent cat, disposable paper nappies must be used and changed frequently. The fur around the hind parts must be sponged clean and dried carefully, and in the case of long-haired breeds, it may be advisable to clip the hair very short in this region. Even a very ill cat will try to use a sanitary tray if it has the strength, and one should always be provided, and the contents changed frequently; paper tissues or cat litter should be used instead of earth, ashes, peat, or sawdust, which soil and stick to the coat. Daily grooming is important, a gentle combing of the hair and the washing of soiled areas around the mouth, chin, chest, and tail. In respiratory illness, the nostrils and eyelids become caked with discharge and must be bathed with warm saline solution, dried, and a little petroleum jelly applied to prevent soreness. Talcum powder can be used in the coat and around the chin and tail regions to keep the hairs parted and clean, and very sick cats certainly appear to appreciate these gentle ministrations. Some infections affect the eyes and eye-ointment has to be applied. The eye must first be cleaned with saline solution, and the ointment placed carefully along the inside of the lower lid with the nozzle of the tube. The eye is then allowed to blink shut and the ointment is naturally spread over the front of the eye.

Cats suffering from bronchial and catarrhal infections benefit greatly from inhalations of medicated vapour or even eucalyptus or camphorated oils. The inhalation is made up in the prescribed manner and placed in a deep bowl within a firm-sided large cardboard box with the lid removed. The cat is placed in a mesh carrier or wicker basket and the basket is fitted across the top of the box so that the vapours can penetrate the carrier. A plastic tablecloth or sheet is spread over the box and carrier to keep the vapours in and the cat is allowed to steam for about fifteen minutes. Petroleum jelly should be applied to the eyelids and nostrils before this treatment, which may make these sensitive areas more inflamed. After inhalation treatment the cat will drool and great streamers of catarrh will come from the mouth and nostrils. These should be wiped away and an improvement in breathing will be

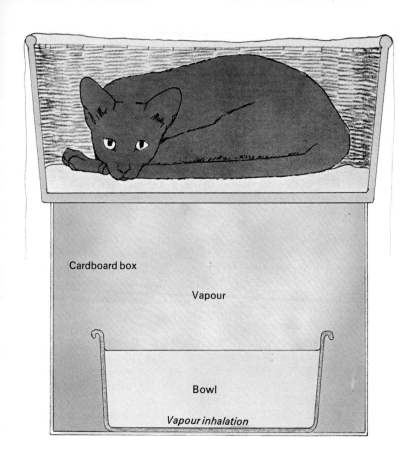

Cardboard box

Vapour

Bowl

Vapour inhalation

immediately apparent. This is an opportune moment to offer some tempting food, and in some cases the first voluntary meal for many days will be accepted.

Home nursing plays a very important part in the recovery of the cat and is equally as important as the antibiotics and medicants prescribed by the veterinary surgeon. Although hard and often distasteful work, it is very rewarding when the long hours of patient care and attention are rewarded by those first tentative, voluntary laps of milk, and the rather unsteady totter to the toilet tray brings the realization that the crisis period has at last been passed, and the chance of a full recovery lies ahead.

Common ailments

Abortion: Caused by rough handling, infection, accident or malnutrition, or by undertaking a long journey in an advanced state of pregnancy. The cat should be provided with a warm box and a water-bowl and she will probably cope with the birth and clean up all the foetuses. It is important for her to be examined by the veterinary surgeon when she has settled down to make sure nothing remains behind to cause infection, but it is not necessary to call him out in the middle of the night as this does not constitute an emergency. If the pregnancy terminates before the fifty-seventh day, the kittens, if born alive, stand very little chance of survival. There is a stronger chance of survival after the fifty-seventh day, but the kittens will need intensive care.

Anaemia: May be *acute* due to internal bleeding, *chronic* due to vitamin deficiency, or following enteritis, or *infectious anaemia* which is a specific disease of cats. Anaemia can also be caused if the cat ingests something toxic, and in all cases the gums are very pale, the cat is listless and any exertion causes a rapid heart-beat and laboured breathing. Veterinary attention with tests to determine the cause is essential.

Bladder: Two conditions affect the bladder of the cat and both require the services of your veterinary surgeon without delay. The first is *cystitis* which causes pain on urination. The urine which may be blood-stained, is passed in tiny quantities at frequent intervals. Occurring mainly in spayed females, antibiotic treatment soon effects a cure. *Bladder stones,* more common in the neutered male cat, are caused when sandy deposits form in the urine and block the tiny urethral passage. The cat strains but cannot urinate and the bladder rapidly swells. This painful condition is classed as a full emergency and professional help should be sought immediately.

Conjunctivitis: Simple infections, dust, smoke, or injury may all give rise to *conjunctivitis* or inflammation of the eyelids, which is often made worse by the cat's constant rubbing at the area in an attempt to relieve irritation. Saline solution, made by boiling a pint of water and adding one teaspoon of salt, then allowed to cool, is ideal for bathing the eye which should be shielded from bright lights. If the condition does not improve within three days, veterinary advice should be sought.

Constipation: Lethargy and vomiting is often the first sign of constipation in a normally healthy cat. A too-dry diet, lack of exercise, or change in routine may cause constipation. Wads of hair ingested during the spring moult, may also block the bowel. Starvation, lots of liquids, and a dose of liquid paraffin or olive oil should ease the condition. If it does not, then a veterinary examination must be made as soon as possible.

Cysts: These usually appear on older cats, either on the ears, due to scratching when ear mites are present, or on the eyelids. Cysts can also appear on the mammary glands, on the testes of old males, and occasionally between the toes. They must never be pricked or treated with home remedies, and the veterinary surgeon will decide whether they should be left alone or removed surgically.

Dermatitis: Inflammation of the skin can be caused by parasites, an incorrect diet, or a reaction to drugs. If no parasites are apparent, only the veterinarian can determine the cause and effect a cure. Calomine lotion should be applied sparingly to the sore regions and allowed to dry into the skin before gently brushed off and the cat prevented from licking the areas if possible. Professional help should be sought as soon as possible.

Diarrhoea: If, after a complete starvation diet, your cat continues to pass liquid faeces for more than twenty-four hours, he should be taken to the veterinary surgeon with a sample of the diarrhoea. In kittens, diarrhoea is usually caused by diet change or a heavy worm burden and can be extremely serious if neglected. Kittens with diarrhoea must *not* be wormed until the condition is under control, and should be given egg-white and boiled water only, to rest the stomach. Diarrhoea in kittens is often due to stress caused by a change in environment. Withhold all food for a few hours, then give only meat, boiled fish, or chopped hard-boiled egg and plenty of drinking water which should correct the condition. Milky food can be resumed when the faeces return to normal.

Drooling: This is distressing to the owner when great streams of saliva drip from the cat's mouth. It is usually caused after a dose of unpleasant medicine, or when some object is wedged across the palate or between the teeth. Tartar build-up and decaying teeth can also cause drooling, and the mouth must be examined so that the appropriate action can be taken. When accompanied by discharge from the eyes and nose, one of the upper respiratory diseases is indicated, and the veterinary surgeon should be called immediately.

Eclampsia: Convulsions in kittens may be due to worms, ear-mite infestation, or teething troubles, and the kitten should be picked up in a thick towel and put into a well-padded cat carrier in a warm dark spot until it recovers. Convulsions in kittens are not serious unless they recur, when a complete physical examination should be given. In adults, eclampsia is serious and in pregnant or nursing queens is due to calcium deficiency. If not treated without delay it can prove fatal, so is classed as an emergency.

Eczema: Skin diseases must be treated by the veterinary surgeon, who, firstly, has to determine whether they are due to parasitic infestation or are eczema. Eczema can be due to flea-bite, when the cat's skin is sensitized to the flea and a dermatitis sets up, which the cat scratches until its whole body is a mass of infected and festering skin. Nutritional exzema is often caused by feeding too much fish; and hormonal eczema appears in neutered cats for no apparently obvious reason. The difficulty with eczema is in determining the cause and prescribing the right treatment, and many frustrating months may be spent before the cat returns to normal. A good diet, careful grooming of the bald and sore patches, and a jacket, or Elizabethan collar to prevent the cat pulling out more and more hair all help when used in conjunction with the injections and tablets administered by the veterinary surgeon.

Enteritis: Feline Infectious Enteritis is a virus disease of the cat. There are several very effective vaccines available, and these should be given to young kittens of twelve weeks or so and regularly boosted. A cat with F.I.E. seems perfectly normal one moment, then becomes depressed, sits hunched up, coat staring. This behaviour is soon followed by attacks of vomiting. The temperature will probably be around 40 °C. Dehydration quickly sets in and the cat seems to lose weight and shrink. Death follows usually within twenty-four hours, but if the internal damage and dehydration can be combated and the cat has a strong will to live it is possible to save him. Veterinary attention is, of course, vital, plus dedicated care and attention. The disease is highly contagious and can be spread by human contact as well as from cat to cat. If the cat dies of this infection, do not buy another kitten for six months, and be sure to have it vaccinated before it is brought into your home.

'Flu: More correctly known as *Feline Viral Rhinotracheitis* or *Pneumonitis,* 'cat 'flu' viruses attack the upper respiratory areas in the cat and symptoms vary from mild sneezing and watery eyes to a severe infection with ulceration of the mouth and throat, red, swollen, and streaming eyes and a completely blocked nose. No case of 'cat 'flu' should be treated lightly, and early veterinary treatment is essential, for if neglected, the infection may gain a strong hold and take months to clear up completely. Many cats becoming affected die despite care and antibiotic treatment. Some are left with blocked sinuses or wet eyes for life. If your cat does get "flu', keep him at home and away from other cats, and do not allow friends who own cats to touch him, for this is a most infectious disease, against which there is no really effective inoculation to date (*see Home Nursing*).

Gingivitis: This is inflammation of the gums, but may be a symptom of something more serious, such as enteritis or 'flu. The first sign of trouble is the cat's loss of appetite, and upon examination of the mouth, a red line is apparent along the join between gums and teeth. Veterinary treatment is necessary, plus home treatment of gum massage with salt water or a weak hydrogen peroxide solution on cotton buds. Needless to say, the cat does not like the treatment, but with perseverance the condition may be cleared before it becomes ulcerative. Soft foods must be given while the mouth is sore, plus a course of Vitamin B complex.

Haws: The third eyelid or Nictitating Membrane in the cat sweeps across the eyeball from the inner corner when the eyes close. Normally it goes back out of sight, but if the cat has worms or is incubating some infectious disease, the haws may remain partially across the eye. This can happen when the cat is particularly tired, after a cat show or when returning from stud, but if the condition persists for more than twenty-four hours, veterinary advice should be sought and the cause determined. Bathing, or the application of ointments, is useless.

Kidney Disease: The first symptoms of kidney disease are a noticeable increase in water consumption, followed by increased urination, occasionally accompanied by straining. Later the cat will lose weight, have bad breath, and be listless. The veterinary surgeon will take a blood and urine sample to determine the exact disease and will treat the patient accordingly. Cats with kidney problems should be kept safely indoors and will have daily vitamin and 'kidney' pills. They must usually be fed a special diet to keep the kidneys functioning and must always have access to drinking water.

Liver Disease: If the cat's eyes change colour and the gums appear yellow, he has jaundice and this is symptomatic of a liver disorder. The only chance of survival for the cat is immediate and expert veterinary attention, but unfortunately the success rate in these cases is very low.

Mammary Tumours: Found on female cats, normally those which have never had kittens, but also occasionally on males, *mammary tumours* are small hard lumps on the under body between the nipples. They grow very quickly and it is imperative that they are examined by the veterinary surgeon without delay. He will recommend surgical removal if necessary.

Pneumonia: This can follow an upper respiratory infection or may be a primary condition, but in either case the cat will have laboured breathing, using the abdominal muscles, rather than the chest muscles, to pump the lungs. The cat must have complete rest and be confined to a small pen if possible, with a warm bed, toilet tray and constant temperature. The crisis period usually lasts about a week and the cat takes at least a month to recover. Veterinary treatment consists of antibiotic injections and possibly a saline drip to prevent dehydration. Home nursing is of the utmost importance and it must be remembered that a relapse could occur at any time during the convalescent period.

Pyometra: Although it is an unusual condition in the cat it is a very serious one and must receive veterinary attention without delay. *Pyometra* or *metritis* is an infected womb, and the uterus is filled with pus. The cat drinks a great deal and may vomit, she may also have an unpleasant discharge from the vagina, and must be admitted to the surgery for the removal of ovaries and uterus immediately the condition is diagnosed.

Rabies: Considered to be the most painful disease known to man, rabies can be prevented by inoculation. Cat owners living in rabid areas should have their pets inoculated as kittens and regularly boosted. Those who live on islands such as Britain or

Hawaii, which are rabies-free, must adhere to the stringent quarantine regulations on animal importation that are designed to prevent this dread disease.

Rectal Impaction: Matted hair or a lot of minced bone in the diet may cause *rectal impaction* in the cat. The cat is listless and strains to pass his motion without success and on inspection a mass of dried faeces can be seen. The area should be carefully washed and a suppository inserted, plus a dose of liquid paraffin by mouth, but if there is no success in clearing the blockage within four or five hours, veterinary attention must be obtained. The diet should be adjusted so that plenty of bulk is included, and some laxative food such as raw liver should be fed twice a week.

Snuffles: *Rhinitis* or *snuffles* often follows a severe bout of 'flu which was not treated in its early stages. Thick catarrhal discharge fills the nose of the cat and is snuffled and sneezed out. Occasionally the discharge is blood-stained and after sneezing a nose-bleed follows. Snuffles is difficult to cure and relapses occur, usually during periods of stress, such as a few days in the boarding cattery. Cats with *chronic rhinitis* cannot be allowed the run of the house because of the mess made by the discharge. Fresh air and a well-balanced diet occasionally help the condition.

Thrombus: The cat becomes suddenly depressed and resents handling, and one or both the hind legs seem to drag behind him. The legs feel cold to the touch and the condition is caused by a blood clot forming in the artery that sends the blood supply to the hind legs. It is vital that the cat is taken without delay to the veterinary surgeon for an immediate operation to remove the clot and restore the circulation in order to save the cat's life. Even so, *thrombus* is usually fatal.

Ulcerative Glossitis: The cat is listless and sits with his mouth slightly open. He cannot eat and may sit by his water bowl wanting to drink but unable to bring himself to do so. His breath is offensive, his tongue sore and deeply ulcerated and the area between his mouth and nostrils may also be ulcerated and bleeding. *Ulcerative glossitis* usually affects young cats and early veterinary treatment is successful. While sick he must be syringe-fed with liquid foods and kept clean and warm.

Zoonoses: Some diseases can be transmitted from the cat to man and from time to time the media decide to put a general alarm call out to the public about the dangers of keeping pets. The first rule in pet keeping is one of hygiene, and children should be taught to keep their hands away from their faces during and after handling their pets. Animal plates should be washed after each meal and never with the family's dishes. The cat must be kept free from internal and external parasites, and toilet trays kept in the home must be changed and sterilized daily.

Common parasites

The Flea is the most common of all parasites found living on the domestic cat, and several different types may breed at the same time in the cat's coat. They live by puncturing the skin and sucking blood, and when present in large numbers, have a severely debilitating effect on the cat's health. Some cats are allergic to the flea-bite itself, and after an infestation, lose areas of hair along the spine and around the head area. As the flea also acts as an intermediate host to the tape-worm, it is important that it is never allowed to gain a hold on the cat and its living quarters. Clusters of tiny dark-brown granules in the fur are the first signs of flea infestation in the pet cat, and mark the spots where the flea has fed on blood and subsequently excreted. A search around the head, armpits and base of the spine will soon reveal the adult fleas which move quickly and so are difficult to catch. To satisfactorily control an outbreak of fleas, it is necessary to know a little of their life cycle. The eggs are laid on the cat's coat, but being hard, small, and spherical, soon roll off and are deposited into tiny crevices in carpets, furnishings, and bedding. The eggs eventually hatch out as tiny maggot-like larvae which feed on particles of household dust and debris. The adult fleas emerge from the chrysalis stage and wait for the next warm body to pass by, whether it be a human, a dog, or a cat, when they jump quickly aboard, taking the first opportunity to bite the skin for a meal. Thorough vacuuming of all floor areas and furniture, and the careful laundering of bedding will help to eradicate eggs, larvae, and chrysalids. An all-out attack on the adult fleas must be waged by bathing or dusting the cat, taking extreme care that the products used are not toxic, and are specifically for use on cats. Some products designed for treatment of dogs are quite effective and harmless when used on that species but may prove fatal if used on your cat. Regular combing of the cat with a very fine-toothed comb will help keep him free from flea infestation and it is comforting to know that the cat flea (*Ctenocephalides felis*) will not live on human beings !

Lice are also occasionally found on the pet cat, and are fairly difficult to clear, because the eggs are cemented on to individual hairs, and are resistant to treatment. The adult lice attach themselves by their mouth-parts to the cat's skin, and form themselves into small clusters, mainly in the head region. These can be picked off with eyebrow tweezers and dropped into a saucer of disinfectant. The eggs can be groomed out of the coat with a very fine-toothed comb. The veterinary surgeon will supply a special medicated shampoo with which the cat can be bathed at fort-nightly intervals until all signs of the pests have been removed. During treatment, a disposable cardboard box and newspapers should be provided as bedding for the cat, changed, and burnt daily to prevent re-infection.

Harvest Mites are sometimes noticed on cats, usually towards the end of a long dry summer, and are minute orange-red creatures, found in clusters on the ears and forehead, and sometimes between the toes and around the claw bed. Extremely irritating, these mites cause the cat to scratch violently and the affected areas quickly become raw and weeping. Luckily, dusting the localized patches with an insecticidal powder, or washing the paws with a mildly medicated soap quickly despatches the harvest mites and relieves the irritation.

Sheep Ticks are rarely found on coats, and are often mistaken for warts, as when gorged with blood they resemble bluish-grey baked beans, hanging pendulously from the skin. If found on the cat, a tiny drop of methylated spirit or surgical spirit must be introduced around the mouth parts of the tick where they enter the skin, to make them relax their grip. Then the whole tick can be carefully lifted free with tweezers, and destroyed. The spirit will sting the cat, which must be held firmly, as it is important that the mouth-parts are removed entirely, any parts breaking off and remaining embedded in the skin will produce a wound which will prove resistant to treatment, taking up to four weeks to heal completely.

Maggot Infestation is generally only seen in long-haired cats following a bout of sickness or diarrhoea, when small plugs of faecal material remain matted in the coat around the rear end. A blow fly then lays its eggs in this mat and within four days the horrified owner will notice the cat's extreme distress and agitated behaviour, and see a large cluster of maggots which have hatched out. Obviously this condition causes distress to both cat and owner, and the maggots must be picked off with tweezers and destroyed, then the affected area must be carefully clipped of fur and the red and angry area treated with a soothing antiseptic.

Roundworms are very common, especially in young kittens, and are very debilitating, living as they do on blood drawn from the host

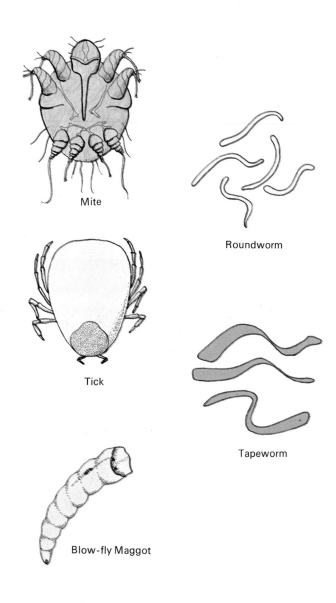

Mite

Roundworm

Tick

Tapeworm

Blow-fly Maggot

Parasites that can infect a cat

and migrating through various organs of the body, shedding toxic waste products as they go, and upsetting the animal's entire system. Roundworms are 2-5 inches long, dull cream in colour, and may be vomited or passed out in the motions. Sometimes, however, no worms are seen, but the cat or kitten has a dull coat and eyes and never appears a hundred per cent healthy. Unless a heavy infestation is present, no further complications arise, but conscientious cat owners dose their pets for roundworm at six-monthly intervals. Roundworm eggs dry out away from the host animal and can remain in a torpid state for up to five years, then when picked up on the paws, and swallowed during the cat's ablutions, the ingested egg develops, migrates through the bowel wall, into the lung or liver tissue, and undergoes further changes before returning to the bowel as an adult worm. Only when in the bowel can the worm be attacked by the worming preparation, and regular dosing under veterinary supervision is essential to ensure the complete eradication of these parasites from a heavily infected cat or kitten.

Tape Worms are rarely seen in the cat and are first noticed when dry segments are passed out in the faeces, looking like flattened rice grains. Cats with tapeworm are usually thin and have recurring bouts of diahrroea, and, occasionally, a persistent dry cough. The coat will feel harsh to the touch and the general condition will be poor. The head of the tape worm is buried deep in the bowel wall, and the segments which contain the minute egg are constantly cast off and passed out in the faeces. These tiny eggs are ingested by fleas and undergo changes within the body of the host flea, only infecting another cat when the flea carrying the parasite is in turn ingested, so by keeping your cat free from fleas, you also keep him free from tape worm. To treat the tape worm in the cat requires a rather drastic dosing in order to kill the very resistant head section. This is always a job for the veterinary surgeon, who can examine and weigh the cat, and administer the exact dose of vermicide required.

Mange Mites are very contagious, but luckily quite easy to control. Two sorts attack the domestic cat, sarcoptic and demodectic, both causing intense irritation as they live within the layers of the skin, tunnelling out channels where they breed. The weeping lesions are caused by the cat's scratching at the irritating areas, and secondary bacterial infections invade the skin, causing thickening and formation of large scabs. Mange mites breed on the host animal, mainly around the head and ears, and are most active, thus causing the greatest irritation, in warm conditions — in the summertime and when the animal is curled up at night. Lack of rest causes a severe and sudden loss of condition in the infected cat, and the head and ears soon become encrusted and sore from the constant scratching. The veterinary surgeon takes skin scrapings to determine the identity of the pest under the microscope, then prescribes the correct dressings, which if applied correctly and at the proper intervals, will effect a complete cure within about three weeks. During this time, however, the cat must be confined, and all bedding and hair groomed from his coat must be burnt to prevent a spread of the insects.

Ear mites are fairly common in the cat, and are very small insects, just visible to the naked eye, which live in the ear, irritating the lining and causing the cat to scratch and rub at its ears, with great shaking of the head from time to time. The first sign of infestation with ear mites is usually the twitching and flicking of the affected ear. No further symptoms are apparent for a few days, then the more noticeable scratching begins. The mites live and breed right down in the ear canal where their burrowing habits set up large inflamed areas. Their excreta forms a brownish crust under which they thrive, and it is the extrusion of this matter into the outer part of the ear which usually prompts the owner to have the condition treated. Special lotion must be introduced into the ear canal at prescribed intervals, and it is essential that the treatment is carried out under veterinary supervision so that the delicate lining of the ear is not damaged. If not treated, an infestation of ear mites will thoroughly depress the cat, and, in cases of extreme neglect, surgery has been necessary to re-open the ear canal.

Ringworm is a fungus disease of the skin which is very serious in the pet cat, as it can be transmitted to human beings. Small round lesions are noticed in the fur, with what looks like cigarette ash scattered over their surfaces. These lesions are first apparent on the head and on the inside of the forelegs, and when seen, the cat must be taken to the veterinary surgery at the earliest opportunity for a correct diagnosis. If ringworm is confirmed, the cat must be carefully isolated, and all his treatment must be undertaken wearing rubber gloves. A cardboard box with newspaper lining should be used for bedding and burnt after a few days to be replaced by another, and hair groomed out must be carefully gathered and also burnt. Internal treatment is now available for ringworm, and is given in tablet form, and the hair is clipped away from the lesions so that ointment can be applied locally. Short-haired cats prove easier to clear than long-haired cats, but with patience and dedicated care, the fungus will be completely eradicated.

Holiday and travel

One aspect of cat-care not always considered when a kitten is acquired, is the problem of finding adequate holiday accommodation for him every year, for even if the holiday is only for a few days, a cat must not be left to fend for itself. In a sudden emergency, a fully grown cat could be left safely shut in the home with a supply of complete dried cat-diet and a large bowl of water, plus toilet tray and warm bed, but it should not be left for more than thirty-six hours. If you are away for a longer period, and there is no one available to provide regular meals and attention, it is essential that a licensed and approved boarding cattery is contacted well in advance of the departure date, and the cat booked in for the duration of the holiday.

There are many boarding catteries, some good, some bad, and many which are mediocre, and it is up to the individual owner to search out and select a cattery which offers the service he requires for his pet. Animal societies and veterinary surgeons will often recommend catteries which they know offer good accommodation and expert care, and newspapers and the Yellow Pages carry advertisements. Some catteries, however, enjoy heavy bookings all year because of their high standards, and these may not need or care to advertise their service, being assured of continuity of boarders by the recommendation of their existing clientele. Prices vary considerably, and it is usually true to say that you get what you pay for. Heated catteries with large and well-planned runs obviously cost much more to set up and maintain than a series of rabbit hutches in a converted garage, and individual diets are more costly to prepare than soaked cat biscuit.

Having found a suitable cattery near at hand, it should be ascertained that the premises are licensed with the relevant local authority, and then a visit should be made to have a look round and to enquire about diet and other requirements. It is usually important to book well in advance to avoid disappointment, especially at peak holiday times, and you may be asked to pay the fees in advance, or to leave a deposit against cancellation. Most good catteries insist upon current vaccination against Feline Panleucopaenia and you may be asked to produce the vaccination certificate. Entire males are not usually accepted into normal boarding catteries, although some establishments which also have breeding facilities may make a stud house available for a registered stud male if the booking is made well in advance. If your cat needs special diet, medication, extra grooming, is convalescing after an accident, or is pregnant or nursing kittens, you will obviously expect to pay extra fees.

Outdoor catteries, which are far superior to indoor catteries in that the risk of the spread of upper respiratory infections is greatly reduced, should have individual huts or chalets of a minimum size 3ft x 4ft x 3ft, each with a paved or concreted run securely wired in, with each run-door opening into a safety area to prevent escape. The chalets should be made of wood as this is a warm material, and should be smoothly lined, painted, and washable inside, with room for a toilet tray, bed, and dishes. There should be an adequate service door, plus a small cat door giving access to the run, and a window so that the cat has plenty of light, even on rainy days. For winter boarding some form of heating, such as an infra-red emitter, should be installed. The cattery should not have an unpleasant odour and should present a workmanlike appearance. Any cats present should look well-fed and contented, and you should make certain that your cat's requirements as regards food, grooming, and care will be met, that there is a veterinary surgeon on call, and that the premises are not left unattended at any time.

After making your booking, be sure to deliver and collect on the days and at the times you have agreed, as many catteries suffer great inconvenience when cats booked out are not collected until a day or so later, and the incoming cat has arrived to take up residence in that particular chalet. If you cut short your holiday and return early, do not be surprised if the proprietor does not offer to give you a rebate on your boarding fees. Most catteries rely on a very short season and therefore need to have each chalet full through the whole of that period in order to stay in business. By returning home a few days early and collecting your cat, you leave a chalet which cannot be re-let at short notice.

Make sure that you confine your cat to the house well before the time comes to set off for the cattery — cats have an uncanny knack of disappearing at the crucial moment. Take him in a secure container, either a proper wicker or wire-mesh carrier, a disposable carrier from the pet store, or even a safe zipped-top bag. In an emergency, a strong pillow case may be used, the cat being popped inside and the top twisted round. Many cats escape each year and become strays, for if an adequate container is not provided, when the car door is opened, the cat, which may be unsettled in a strange area, may often disappear without trace, much to the anguish of his owners.

Be sure to take your cat's own bed to the cattery, and a few toys so that he will not feel too fretful at being left. Take an old blanket and do not wash it just before the boarding period as this destroys the smells of home which are comforting to the cat. Bear in mind that some cats have lapses of good behaviour when in strange surroundings, so do not give him the baby's best cot blanket, for he could well use his bed for toilet purposes and the proprietors may find it necessary to burn the bedding. An old sweater is best, given to him at home in his basket for about two weeks before the holiday, then if he does eat it or mess it up, no real harm is done. You will probably be asked to sign some form of indemnity and pay your account on admission, then the cat will be given a thorough check over for any signs of parasites, or symptoms of infection, before being put in his chalet. If he becomes ill while boarding, the attending veterinary surgeon will be called in. An emergency number or address can be left with the cattery in case of

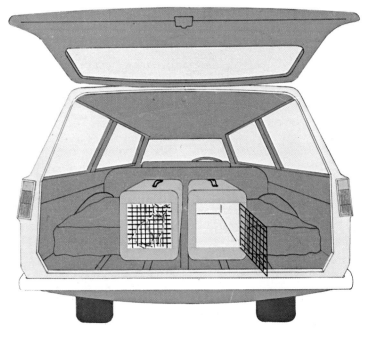

Carrying the cat: these cages are constructed from light-weight fibreglass

accident to the cat, or even to yourself. Your cat, like the majority of feline boarders, will probably go on hunger strike for two or three days, then settle down to enjoy the pleasant routine of cattery life. When you return, he should look fit and well, and be very pleased to see you, but probably rubbing all around the legs of the proprietors as well!

Great Britain has very strict quarantine restrictions on animals brought in from abroad. The restrictions were introduced to prevent the possible spread of the dreadful disease Rabies.

Cats do not take kindly to the six-month-long solitary confinement in quarantine kennels, no matter how well and expertly these are run, and much thought should be exercised before deciding to subject any cat or kitten to this ordeal. Other countries have varying degrees of quarantine and import restrictions, and if intending to transport a cat from one country to another, enquiries should be made of one's veterinary surgeon as to the certification and restrictions applicable.

Some cats love to ride in cars and sit happily gazing out of the window on even the longest journeys, but others are very disturbed by the motion, and dribble and pant, becoming more and more agitated. Such cats must be confined within a carrier and taken on frequent short journeys in order to try to accustom it to travelling if such trips are to be a necessary part of its life. Training to a collar or harness and lead is also a good idea for cats which have to travel frequently, so that they may be safely restrained when getting in and out of the car, and when windows are open.

Cats are permitted to travel on trains with their owners, but should be in a basket, and if they are noisy, or the train is crowded, they may have to travel in the freight van. Basketed cats are also allowed on buses, and, for short internal air trips, cats are allowed as excess baggage and may travel in the cabin at the discretion of the cabin crew. On longer overseas flights, however, they travel as cargo in a pressurized hold, and must be loaded in specially designed, wooden, crushproof carriers. Whenever possible, cats should be accompanied on their travels, and sedation, even when carried out under the instructions of a veterinary surgeon, can have such adverse effects as it wears off, that it is recommended only as a very last resort.

Index